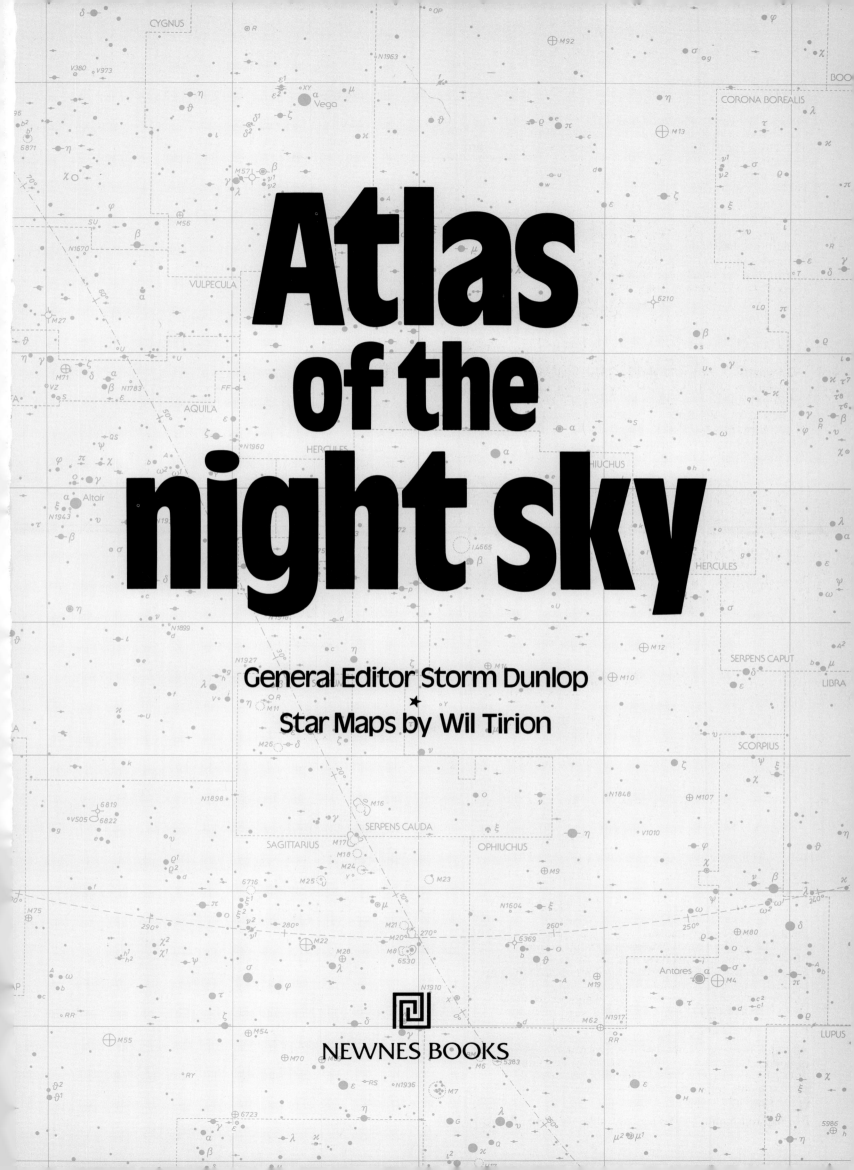

Atlas of the night sky

General Editor Storm Dunlop

★

Star Maps by Wil Tirion

NEWNES BOOKS

Acknowledgements

Artwork
Epoch 2000.0 star charts pages 12–23 – Wil Tirion
Constellation maps pages 24–67 and diagrams pages 4, 5, 6, 7, 68 (centre right), 69, 70, 71, 74, 77 (bottom left) – Oxford Illustrators Ltd
Moon map (page 72–73) and diagrams 75–76, 77 (bottom right) 79 – Tom MacArthur
Drawing of Jupiter (page 77 centre) by kind permission of Dr R. J. McKim, Peterborough.
Drawing of Sun spots (page 68 centre left) – Harold Hill, Wigan, Lancashire
The presentation of the constellation diagrams have been adapted from the *Concise Guide in Colour: Constellations* by Josef Klepesta and Antonin Rükl

Photographs
W. Cobley, Cleethorpes – 69 top right, bottom left; Peter Gill – 5; Hale Observatories – California Institute of Technology and Carnegie Institute of Washington – 9; Hale Observatories – Charles T. Kowal – 11 centre; Hale Observatories, Pasadena, California – 11 top; Lick Observatory University of California – 70; Royal Astronomical Society – Royal Greenwich Observatory – 68; Royal Observatory, Edinburgh – 10; Science Photo Library – Ronald E. Royer 79; D. A. R. Simmons, Glasgow 69 top left, bottom right; University of Arizona, Tucson – Stephen Larson – 78.

Published by Newnes Books,
a Division of The Hamlyn Publishing Group Limited
84–88 The Centre, Feltham, Middlesex, England
and distributed for them by The Hamlyn Publishing Group Limited, Rushden, Northants, England.
© Newnes Books, a Division of The Hamlyn Publishing Group Limited 1984

ISBN 0 600 35113 0

Printed and bound by Poligrafici Calderara s.p.a. Bologna, Italy

Contents

Introduction — Celestial co-ordinates

It is essential for astronomers to be able to specify the exact positions of celestial objects, whether they are the so-called 'fixed' stars, planets, or other bodies. The method which is used is very similar to the system of latitude and longitude employed on the surface of the Earth (and nowadays also on other bodies in the Solar System). It is possible because, although we now know it to be an illusion, the heavens appear to be a sphere centred on the observer. With the rotation of the Earth all celestial objects appear to pass across the sky once a day. This provides north and south celestial poles (around which everything else appears to rotate), a celestial equator, in the same plane as the Earth's equator, and circles of declination (Dec) – the stellar equivalent of latitude on Earth. The latter are specified by their angles north (+) or south (−) of the celestial equator, which is regarded as having a declination of 0°.

The provision of the other co-ordinate, right ascension (RA) – the equivalent of longitude – is a little more complicated. It can be measured along the celestial equator, and as the Sun appears to take a day to pass round through 360°, it is convenient to use measurements of time (hours, minutes, or if one is being very precise, seconds) to describe right ascension ($24^h = 360°$, $1^h = 15°$, $1^m = 15'$, etc.). But where should that measurement start? The answer was to use the apparent path of the Sun in the sky, the ecliptic. This is tilted at about 23.5° to the plane of the celestial equator, due to the actual tilt of the Earth's rotational axis to the plane of its orbit around the Sun. At two points the ecliptic crosses the celestial equator, at the equinoxes, when day and night have equal length. The one in spring, the vernal equinox, when the Sun moves from south to north across the equator, was chosen as the point from which right ascension would be measured. This, the

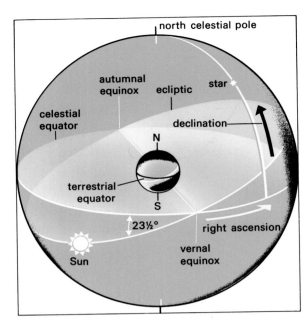

The position of an object on the sky is specified by right ascension, measured eastwards around the celestial equator from the vernal equinox, and declination, measured towards the northern or southern celestial poles.

It takes 25 800 years for the celestial poles to complete their paths around the poles of the ecliptic. In the north (shown here) the centre is in Draco, and in the other hemisphere it lies in the constellation of Dorado, close to the Large Magellanic Cloud.

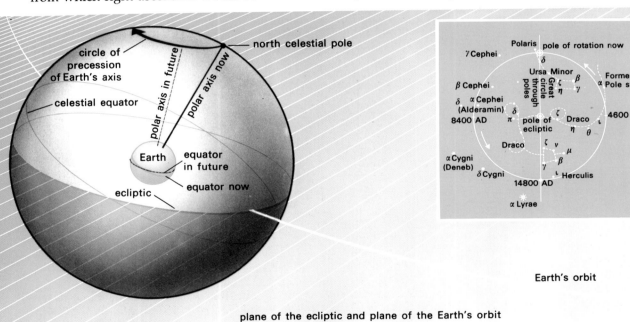

At present precession has caused the Earth's rotational axis to point towards the bright star Polaris, which forms a useful guide to positions in the northern sky.

origin of the system of celestial co-ordinates at 0^h (or 24^h) right ascension, 0° declination, is known as the 'First Point of Aries' from the constellation in which it was located. It is sometimes shown by the symbol ♈ , the ancient zodiacal sign for Aries, the Ram.

Charts can now be drawn showing the positions of the stars (and of other objects) quite precisely. Such a position might be RA = $17^h 40^m$, Dec = 28° 30' (the approximate position of the galactic centre). But another complication has to be taken into account. It was discovered by Hipparchos, the Greek astronomer, around 140 B.C. that the position of the equinoxes changes very slowly, but continuously. This effect, known as precession, is caused by the gravitational effects of the Moon and the Sun on the Earth's equatorial bulge. If the bodies lay in the plane of the Earth's equator little would happen, but as the Earth's axis is tilted, the various forces, including the Earth's rotation, cause the axis to swing round in a cone in space. The axis takes about 25 800 years to complete a circuit of the cone.

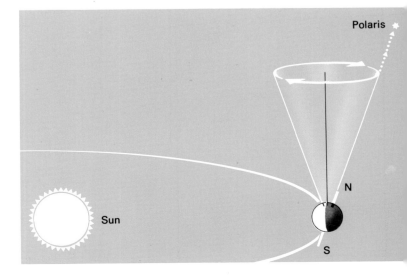

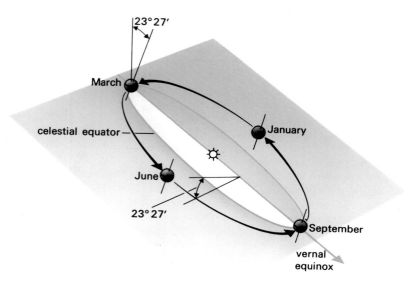

23°27'

March

celestial equator

January

June

23°27'

September

vernal
equinox

The ecliptic not only defines the vernal equinox, and thus the measurement of RA, but as it is the Earth's orbital plane, also serves as a reference for motions of objects in the Solar System.

This means that the position of the vernal equinox is continuously moving westwards against the background of the stars by about 50 seconds of arc per year, and with it the whole system of celestial co-ordinates. It is obviously impossible to keep redrawing charts of the whole sky, so they are usually prepared for certain fixed dates, known as epochs, sometimes 25, but more usually 50 years apart. The epoch is always taken as January 1 of the year concerned – actually 00:00 hours (or midnight) on December 31-January 1.

Some epochs that have been used are 1875.0, 1900.0 and 1950.0. (The figure after the decimal point indicates that the date was the very beginning of the year.) Epoch 2000·0, as in the charts (and all the positions) in this book, is now beginning to be used by most astronomers. To prevent confusion it is usual to state, in parentheses, the actual epoch that applies to a particular position, or set of charts. For example the position of Sirius, the brightest star in the sky, is:

RA = 06^h 41^m 28·7^s Dec = –16° 38' 46" (1950·0) and
RA = 06^h 45^m 08·9^s Dec = –16° 42' 58" (2000·0).

(Precise positions like these are rarely needed by amateur astronomers.)

It is important to remember that just the co-ordinate grid is moving, and that the relative positions of the stars are almost constant. In the case of the nearest stars proper motions, caused by their individual movements in space are detectable with very sensitive methods, but the changes would take many centuries to become of any importance to amateur astronomers. The constellation boundaries are defined in terms of epoch 1875·0 (to agree with an important stellar catalogue) and so these, like the stars, are slowly drifting with respect to the co-ordinate system.

*The altitude of the celestial pole is the same as the observer's latitude on Earth (here drawn approximately equal to the latitude of London, England or Calgary, Alberta). Within this distance of the pole, stars are circumpolar **1** and never set. Stars on the equator **2** rise and set due east and west. Around the other pole stars **3** never rise above the horizon. Stars are highest in the sky where they cross the meridian, which joins the poles and the north and south points of the horizon.*

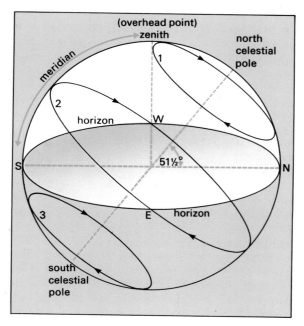

(overhead point)
zenith
north celestial pole
meridian
horizon
W
S
51½°
N
E
horizon
south celestial pole

Northern circumpolar star trails during a two-hour time exposure photograph taken with a fixed camera. The true position of the pole at that date is shown by the centre of all the arcs. Polaris, the bright star, is about 1° from the northern celestial pole.

The amount of precession differs in various parts of the sky. As these extracts from charts of two different epoch show, in the top of Auriga the change in 50 years is quite marked (left epoch 1950·0, *right* epoch 2000·0).

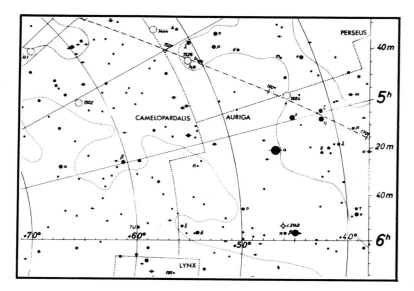

PERSEUS
40m
5^h
CAMELOPARDALIS   AURIGA
20m
40m
70°   60°   50°   40°
6^h
LYNX

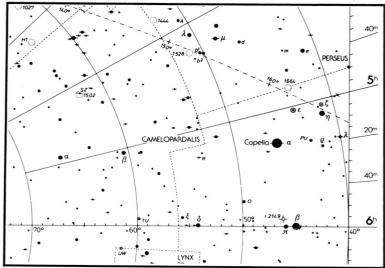

PERSEUS
40m
5^h
CAMELOPARDALIS   Capella
20m
40m
70°   60°   50°   40°
6^h
LYNX

The stars

Stellar distances are difficult to measure because they are so enormous, but the average distance of the Earth from the Sun, the astronomical unit (AU), 149 597 870 km is used as a starting point. As the Earth moves in its orbit, nearby stars show a slight shift in position against distant, background stars, in an effect known as parallax. If the small angles can be measured, ordinary trigonometry gives the distances. To avoid very large numbers the standard unit for stellar distances is the parsec (parallax second, abbreviated pc), the distance at which the radius of the Earth's orbit (1 AU) has an angle of 1 second of arc. It is a distance of 63 240 AU.

Distances are also expressed using the speed of light, just under 300 000 km per second (299 792·458 km/s). One astronomical unit is about 499 light-seconds, and one parsec equals 3·2616 light-years. It is important to remember that a light-year is a measurement of distance, not of time.

Not even the nearest stars are within one parsec of the Solar System. Proxima Centauri lies at about 1·3 pc (4·27 light-years). It is probably a member of a triple system with Alpha Centauri A and B, a little farther distant. The table lists the 20 nearest stars, and the brighter objects are shown on the star charts. As they are close, these objects may show considerable proper motion (page 5). Barnard's star, given in the table, has the exceptionally high rate of 10·25 seconds of arc per annum. When stars are very distant and their parallaxes are too small to be measured, other methods have to be used to make estimates of their distances. These are often based upon statistical information about the brightness and types of stars that are encountered.

Stellar brightness is measured in magnitudes. These were originally a fairly crude guide to the 'importance' of individual stars. (A star of second magnitude appearing about half as bright as one of first magnitude, and so on.) In the last century magnitudes were put on a firm scientific basis and a star of first magnitude now has an intensity exactly 100 times that of a sixth-magnitude object. A one-magnitude difference represents a change in intensity by a factor of about 2·5112.

To the eye, however, one star appears to be twice as bright as another if they have a difference of one magnitude.

It is important to remember that the magnitude scale works 'backwards' and that higher numbers designate fainter stars. When the magnitude scale was finally established it was found that some of the very brightest stars had to be given zero and negative magnitudes for them to fit into the scheme. The twenty brightest stars given in the table include 4 with negative magnitudes.

The apparent magnitudes of stars (as seen from Earth) may be actual differences in brightness, or simply a result of their various distances. If a star's distance is known, its magnitude may be adjusted to obtain the value that it would have at the standard distance of 10pc (about 32·6 light-years). The

The nearest stars. With three exceptions these are all fainter than the Sun. Red and white dwarfs are so faint that they can only be detected in the immediate neighbourhood of the Solar System. 'A' and 'B' indicate the members of binary systems.

The twenty nearest stars				
star	apparent visible magnitude m_v	absolute visible magnitude M_v	spectral class	distance (pc)
Proxima				
Centauri C	11.05	15.45	M5	1.31
Alpha Centauri A	−0.01	4.3	G2	1.34
Alpha Centauri B	1.33	5.69	K5	1.34
Barnard's Star	9.54	13.25	M5	1.81
Wolf 359	13.53	16.68	M8	2.33
HD 95735	7.50	10.49	M2	2.49
Sirius A	−1.45	1.41	A1	2.65
Sirius B	8.68	11.56	WD*	2.65
UV Ceti A	12.45	15.27	M5	2.72
UV Ceti B				
	10.6	13.3	M4	2.90
Ross 248	12.29	14.8	M6	3.15
ε Eridani	3.73	6.13	K2	3.30
L789–6	12.18	14.60	M7	3.30
Ross 128	11.10	13.50	M5	3.32
61 Cygni A	5.22	7.58	K5	3.40
61 Cygni B	6.03	8.39	K7	3.40
ε Indi	4.68	7.00	K5	3.44
Procyon A	0.35	2.65	F5	3.50
Procyon B	10.7	13.0	WD*	3.50
			*white dwarf	

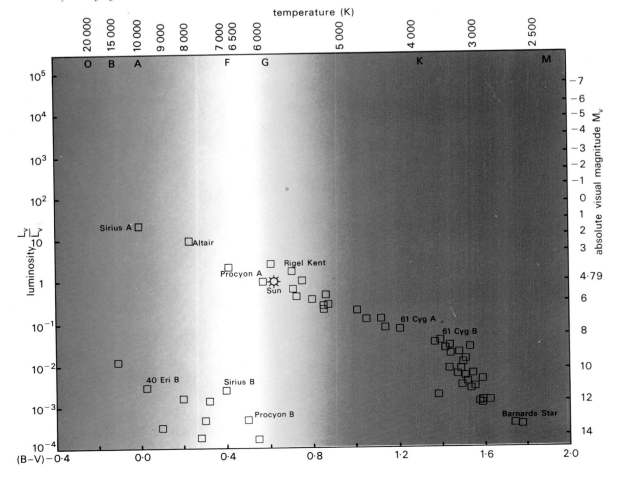

absolute magnitudes (as they are termed) then give an idea of the stars' true luminosity.

Some stars appear quite strikingly coloured. Some may appear white or blue/white, such as Rigel (β Orionis) or Vega (α Lyrae), orange, like Aldebaran (α Tauri), or even deep red as the famous 'Garnet Star', μ Cephei. Due to the effects of contrast many double stars appear strongly coloured, Albireo (β Cyg) being probably the most famous example, the stars appearing golden and green to many observers. However, star colours are basically a measurement of temperatures which may range from more than 40 000 K for some bluish-white objects down to 2 500 K for deep red stars.

Stars may also be classified by their spectral type. The classification takes account of various features, such as absorption or emission lines that may be visible, but the classes also give an indication of temperature. The classes were originally lettered in sequence, but now the order has been revised to O (for the hottest stars), B, A, F, G, K, M. (The time-honoured mnemonic is 'Oh, Be A Fine Girl, Kiss Me'.) There are also certain subsidiary classes, occasionally encountered, such as N, R, S, WR, WC, and C (for carbon stars), which indicate specific spectral characteristics. Each major class is subdivided into 10 numbered sub-classes; for example, the Sun is class G2. Additional letters such as e (for emission lines) and p (for peculiarities) may give additional information.

When the absolute magnitude and spectral class (or temperature) of stars are known, they can be plotted on a Hertzsprung-Russell diagram (named after the astronomers who developed it). Most stars lie on a roughly diagonal line, known as the main sequence. We expect hot stars to be highly luminous, but the diagram shows that there are also cool, red stars with high absolute magnitudes. To be radiating so much energy these must be very large and they are known as giants and supergiants. Antares, α Scorpii is a good example of a supergiant. It is about 1000 times the diameter of the Sun and larger than the orbit of Mars. Main-sequence stars are known as dwarfs.

A star's temperature and lifetime are largely governed by its total mass, although chemical composition also plays a part. High-mass stars are hottest and are found at the top left of the main sequence. Any star spends most of its life on the main sequence, its interior nuclear reactions turning hydrogen into helium. When much of the hydrogen has been used it expands to become a giant or supergiant. Later, its energy resources exhausted, it contracts to become a white dwarf – a body the size of the Earth, but containing about a solar mass – or an even more exotic object such as a neutron star or black hole. The higher the star's original mass, the more rapidly it goes through its evolution. At many stages the star is a variable and may show considerable fluctuations in magnitude.

The twenty brightest stars

star		apparent visible magnitude m_v	absolute visible magnitude M_v	spectral class	distance (pc)
Sirius	α CMa	−1.45	+1.41	A1	2.7
Canopus	α Car	−0.73	+0.16	F0	60
Rigel Kent	α Cen	−0.10	+4.3	G2	1.33
Arcturus	α Boo	−0.06	−0.2	K2 p	11
Vega	β Lyr	0.04	+0.5	AO	8.1
Capella	α Aur	0.08	−0.6	G8	14
Rigel	β Ori	0.11	−7.0	B8	250
Procyon	α CMi	0.35	+2.65	F5	3.5
Achernar	α Eri	0.48	−2.2	B5	39
Hadar	β Cen	0.60	−5.0	B1	120
Altair	α Aql	0.77	+2.3	A7	5.0
Betelgeuse	α Ori	0.80	−6.0	M2	200
Aldebaran	α Tau	0.85	−0.7	K5	21
Acrux	α Cru	0.9	−3.5	B2	80
Spica	α Vir	0.96	−3.4	B1	80
Antares	α Sco	1.0	−4.7	M1	130
Pollux	β Gem	1.15	+0.95	K0	11
Fomalhaut	α PsA	1.16	+0.08	A3	7.0
Deneb	α Cyg	1.25	−7.3	A2	500
Mimosa	β Cru	1.26	−4.7	B0	150

The brightest stars in the sky are all more luminous than the Sun. Some are at very great distances but still appear brilliant because of their very high absolute magnitudes.

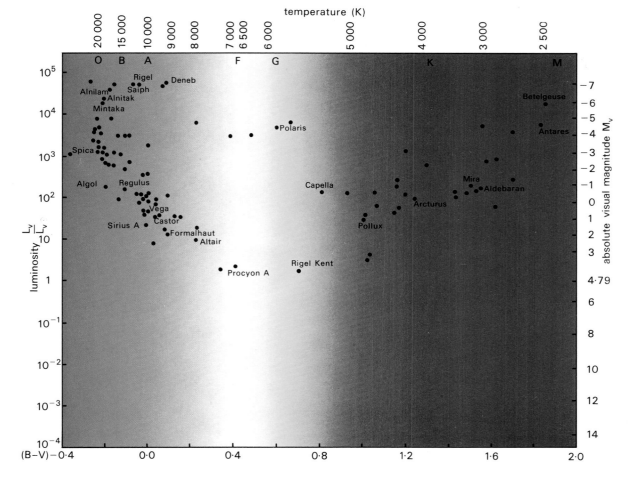

Double stars

Many of the stars are doubles. (They are usually marked on charts by a horizontal bar through the star.) Some are widely-spaced and visible to the naked eye, the most famous probably being Alcor, near Mizar, ζ Ursa Majoris. With even the smallest telescope or binoculars many objects are seen as two or more stars. Some are remarkable for the combinations of colours that they show, others for the number of components that can be seen. However, there are two types of double: optical doubles where two stars happen to lie close to the same line of sight, although really at different distances, and true binary systems where the stars orbit one another. (Multiple objects may, of course, also be of either type.) The relative positions of the optical doubles do not change, except for the stars' individual proper motions. In true binaries the orbital motion may be followed over a number of years. Depending on the apparent shape of the orbits in individual cases, it may sometimes be easy to separate (or resolve) the stars, and at others they may be so close that it is impossible. Some objects (known as spectroscopic binaries) are so close that they cannot be seen as two stars in even the largest telescopes.

Variable Stars

If the orbit of a binary is exactly aligned with the Earth the two stars may pass in front of one another, causing eclipses and changes in brightness. A plot of the magnitude with respect to time produces a light-curve that illustrates the regular behaviour. The most famous eclipsing binary is certainly Algol, β Persei.

There are many other forms of variable stars. All are shown on charts by concentric circles representing the maximum and minimum magnitudes, or a single open circle if they only rise above the charts' limiting magnitude at maximum. Many are single stars that are going through a stage of evolution in which they pulsate. Some are very regular, such as the Cepheid variables, named after the prototype, δ Cephei. Their periods are easily measured, and are related to the absolute magnitudes, known by other means, so these stars form an important method of determining the distances of nearby galaxies. Slightly less regular, but also pulsating, are the long-period variables (LPVs), with periods over 100 days – very commonly about a year. Mira, o Ceti, is a well-known example. The semiregulars (SR) are more erratic, but occasionally show fairly regular changes in magnitude. The RV Tauri stars (RV) are somewhat similar, tending to show alternate deep and shallow minima, which sometimes change places. Stars such as R Coronae Borealis are usually bright, but unpredictably fade and may be dim for many months. Novae (which are actually very close binary systems) and supernovae are brilliant, unpredictable explosions.

Below The number of doubles found in some areas of the sky, as here, makes it obvious that the Sun is a rarity in having no stellar companion.

Bottom Left γ Cas, Algol (β Per), ε and η Aurigae are famous variable stars. RZ Cas (bottom left) is an eclipsing binary that may be observed with binoculars.

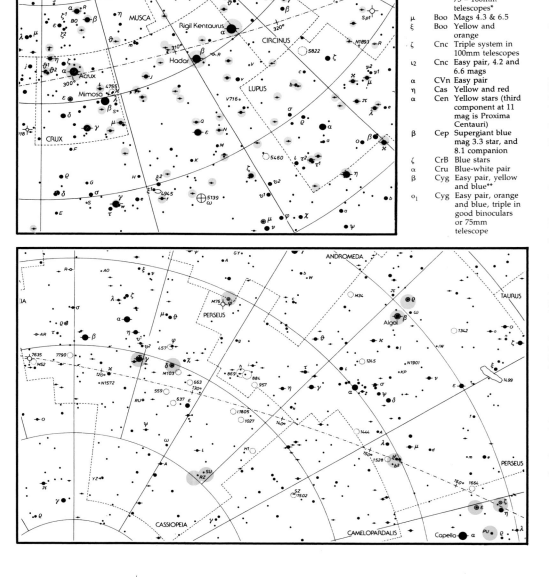

Double stars

Name		Remarks
γ	And	Yellow and blue
ζ	Aqr	White stars in 75 – 100mm telescopes
γ	Ari	White 5ᵐ stars
ε	Boo	Orange and blue-green in 75 – 100mm telescopes*
μ	Boo	Mags 4.3 & 6.5
ξ	Boo	Yellow and orange
ζ	Cnc	Triple system in 100mm telescopes
ι2	Cnc	Easy pair, 4.2 and 6.6 mags
α	CVn	Easy pair
η	Cas	Yellow and red
α	Cen	Yellow stars (third component at 11 mag is Proxima Centauri)
β	Cep	Supergiant blue mag 3.3 star, and 8.1 companion
ζ	CrB	Blue stars
α	Cru	Blue-white pair
β	Cyg	Easy pair, yellow and blue**
o₁	Cyg	Easy pair, orange and blue, triple in good binoculars or 75mm telescope
61	Cyg	Orange stars
γ	Del	Yellow stars
υ	Dra	White 5 mag stars
16–17	Dra	Easy blue-white pair, triple in 75mm
θ	Eri	Easy blue-white pair
o₂	Eri	Triple in 75mm telescopes, mags 4.5, 9.5 (white dwarf) and 11.2 (red dwarf)
α	Gem	(Castor) Blue-white pair and red dwarf (Each star is itself double, but only spectroscopically)
ρ	Her	Easy pair
95	Her	Yellow and white
ε	Hya	Mags 3.5 and 6.9
γ	Leo	Easy pair of yellow stars**
α	Lib	Easy pair, mags 2.9 and 5.3
β	Lyr	Yellow component famous eclipsing binary, blue companion
ε	Lyr	Famous 'double double'. Easy pair, each double in 75 – 100mm**
β	Mon	White triple system
σ	Ori	Triple, blue-white, blue, red. Quadruple in 150mm
ζ	Pav	Red and white stars
η	Per	Orange and blue
β	Sco	Blue-white pair
ν	Sco	Triple Quadruple in 150mm telescope
δ	Ser	White stars
θ	Ser	Easy pair
β	Tuc	Triple
ζ	UMa	(Mizar) Companion (Alcor) visible to good eyes, triple in small telescopes
ξ	UMa	Yellow stars
γ	Vel	Easy blue-white pair, quadruple in 75mm**
γ	Vir	Yellow-white stars**
γ	Vol	Yellowish-white and yellow stars

Variable stars

Name		Remarks
R	And	Long-period variable (about 400 days), mags 6 – 15
ε	Aur	Eclipsing binary (period 27 years), mags 3.5 – 4.5
ζ	Aur	Eclipsing binary (period 32 months), mags 5.0 – 5.5
γ	Cas	Irregular brightening when shell of material is shed
ρ	Cas	Irregular fades, mags 4.1 – 6.2
δ	Cep	Prototype of Cepheid variables (period 5.36 days), mags 3.9 – 5.0
μ	Cep	Semiregular, deep red star, mags 3.6 – 5.1
o	Cet	(Mira) Famous long-period variable (period 330 days, mags 2.0 (on occasions) –10
R	CrB	Normally mag. 6.3, unpredictable fades down to 14 – 15
W	Cyg	Semiregular, mags 6.5 – 8.5, red
χ	Cyg	Long-period variable (period 406 days), extreme range 3.3 – 14.2
β	Lyr	Prototype subclass of eclipsing variable (period 12.91 days), mags 3.3 – 4.2
β	Per	Prototype subclass of eclipsing variables (period 2.87 days), mags 2.1 – 3.4
L₂	Pup	Semiregular, mags 2.6 – 6.0
R	Sct	Semiregular, deep and shallow minima frequently alternate, mags 5.3 – 7.9

Clusters

In some regions of the sky there are denser groupings of stars, some so conspicuous that the individual stars may be seen, and others appearing to the naked eye as just faint, hazy patches. These are not just chance effects (like the optical binaries) but genuine clusters of related stars. Many are identified by the letter M followed by a number, indicating that they were included in the catalogue compiled by the French astronomer Charles Messier, of objects which might be confused with comets. Others carry NGC (*New General Catalogue*) numbers. A few are so bright that they were originally taken to be individual stars, and carry ordinary letter designations.

Open clusters (often known as galactic clusters) vary widely in size and shape. They may contain just a few stars or up to a few hundred. Some are nearby and cover a large area of sky, such as the brilliant Pleiades, and the even larger Hyades, both in Taurus. The total magnitude of others may be no more than a single faint star, so that quite a large telescope may be needed to see them properly.

The stars in open clusters are usually quite young (astronomically speaking), formed recently from an interstellar cloud of dust and gas. As they age the clusters are normally gradually dispersed by the general rotation of the Galaxy. The compact twin clusters in Perseus (the 'Double Cluster', h & χ Persei) for example, are about 12 million years old. Stellar formation is now only occurring in the spiral arms of the Galaxy, so open clusters tend to congregate close to the central line of the Milky Way. As they are young, the stars are often hot, blue objects, although sometimes one or more older, redder stars, may also be included. M35 in Auriga, M44 (Praesepe) in Cancer and particularly the 'Jewelbox' near κ Crucis are a few of the many that show some striking colour contrasts.

Globular clusters are very different. These may contain many thousands of stars (sometimes as many as a million), densely packed into a spherical region of space. Like the galactic clusters some of the brightest are just visible to the naked eye, M13 in Hercules and M22 in Sagittarius are two examples, but ω Centauri, in the southern hemisphere, is the brightest and undoubtedly the finest. Unlike the open clusters, globular clusters are all very far away, and their distances have to be measured in kiloparsecs (kpc) – one kiloparsec is a little over 3 260 light-years. M2 for example, easily visible in binoculars, is more than 12 kpc away. The great distances explain why globular clusters do not appear very bright even though they contain so many stars.

Globular clusters are not distributed along the plane of the Milky Way, in the same way as the open clusters, but instead are strongly concentrated around the galactic centre in Sagittarius. They also contain very old stars and formed very early in the history of the Galaxy, before the disk and spiral arms.

Top *There are several bright open clusters (M16, M26) and globular clusters (M4, M22) in the region of the galactic centre (cross). Note how the open clusters tend to lie along the central plane of the Milky Way.*

Above *A dozen stars, at most, are visible to the naked eye in the Pleiades, M45, but this cluster actually contains 200–300 young stars. Small patches of reflection nebulosity can also be seen.*

Open clusters

cluster	NGC	right ascension h m	declination ° '	apparent magnitude	distance (pc)
h & χ Persei	869, 884	02 22	+57 08	4.2	2 360
M34	1 039	02 42	+42 47	5.6	440
Pleiades (M45)	–	03 47	+24 07	1.3	126
Hyades	–	04 19	+15 37	0.6	45
M38	1 912	05 29	+35 51	7.0	1 320
M36	1 960	05 36	+34 08	6.3	1 260
M37	2 099	05 52	+32 34	6.1	1 280
M35	2 168	06 09	+24 20	5.3	870
Praesepe (M44)	2 632	08 41	+19 41	3.7	158
M67	2 682	08 51	+11 49	6.5	830
K Crucis (Jewelbox)	4 755	12 54	−60 20	5.0	830
M21	6 531	18 05	−22 30	6.8	1 250
M16	6 611	18 19	−13 47	6.6	2 500
M11	6 705	18 51	−06 17	6.3	1 740
M39	7 092	21 32	+48 26	5.1	250

Globular clusters

cluster	NGC	right ascension h m	declination ° '	apparent magnitude	distance (kpc)
47 Tucanae	104	00 24	−72 05	4.0	5.0
ω Centauri	5 139	13 27	−47 19	3.6	5.2
M3	5 272	13 42	+28 23	6.4	10.6
M5	5 904	15 19	+02 05	5.9	8.1
M4	6 121	16 24	−26 31	5.9	4.3
M13	6 205	16 42	+36 27	5.9	6.3
M92	6 341	17 17	+43 09	6.1	7.9
M22	6 656	18 37	−23 56	5.1	3.0
Δ295	6 752	19 11	−59 59	6.2	5.3
M15	7 078	21 30	+12 10	6.4	10.5
M2	7 089	21 34	−00 50	6.3	12.3

Nebulae

Both dust and gas are concentrated along the plane of the Milky Way. In many places the dust is so dense that the light from distant stars is completely obscured. The 'Coalsack' nebula in Crux is the most famous example of one of these dark nebulae, but the 'Great Rift' in Cygnus (which actually runs on down to Scutum and Ophiuchus) has been caused in the same way. In many other areas along the Milky Way the dust lies in delicate threads and wisps, but most of these are difficult to see, except under the darkest skies. Both they, and the general star clouds of the Milky Way, are best examined with low-power binoculars or the naked eye.

Where clouds of dust are close to bright stars they may simply reflect some of the starlight back towards us. As the stars are often brilliant, young, blue/white objects, the reflection nebulae appear blue on photographs, in marked contrast to the pinkish tinge of glowing hydrogen gas found in other nebulae. Unfortunately, few reflection nebulae can be seen visually, but keen-eyed observers may glimpse the Merope nebula in the Pleiades.

In some areas the radiation from hot stars may cause the gas to glow. These are the gaseous, or diffuse nebulae. There are several close to the galactic centre, M8 (the Lagoon Nebula) and M20 (the Trifid Nebula), for example, but the most famous is the great Orion Nebula (M42 & M43) on the opposite side of the sky. The visible filaments cover a large area of the sky, but they are only a small part of an enormous cloud that extends over most of the constellation of Orion. In the heart of the visible nebulosity are the young stars of the Trapezium, θ Orionis, four of which are fairly easy to see.

In the southern Milky Way the nebula around η Carinae (sometimes known as the Key-hole Nebula) is a conspicuous object. (The star itself has occasionally brightened very markedly, being second only to Sirius in 1843. It is now about magnitude 7, but remains a mystery. It has been thought to be very young, but is now believed to be very massive, very old and a possible candidate for a future supernova explosion.) Some of these diffuse nebulae are conspicuous in external galaxies, the most notable being the Tarantula Nebula in the Large Magellanic Cloud (the closest major galaxy), which is actually visible to the naked eye.

Other nebulae are also caused by glowing gas. These are the planetary nebulae, so-named because they have a slight resemblance to planetary disks when seen through small telescopes. They are shells of material from an evolving star, which, after passing through its red giant phase, has cast off much of its outer atmosphere. The stellar remnant is usually seen as a small, hot object in the centre, emitting the radiation that excites the gas. M57 (the Ring Nebula) in Lyra, and M27 (the Dumbbell) in Vulpecula are the most famous examples. Supernova remnants are very similar.

Nebulae						
		RA		Dec. (2000)		
Nebula	Name	h	m	°	'	Type
M76	–	01	42	+51	34	Planetary
M1	Crab	05	35	+22	01	Supernova remnant
M42	Orion Nebula	05	35	−05	23	Diffuse
NGC 2237	Rosette	06	32	−06	42	Diffuse
NGC 2070	Tarantula	06	39	−69	15	Diffuse
NGC 3372	η Carina Nebula	10	45	−59	45	Diffuse
M97	Owl	11	15	+55	02	Planetary
NGC 6543	–	17	59	+66	38	Planetary
M20	Trifid	18	02	−23	02	Diffuse
M8	Lagoon	18	05	−24	20	Diffuse
M17	Omega	18	21	−16	11	Diffuse
M57	Ring	18	54	+33	02	Planetary
M27	Dumbbell	20	00	+22	43	Planetary
NGC 6992	Veil	20	57	+31	42	Supernova remnant
NGC 7000	North America	20	57	+44	20	Diffuse

Below *Cygnus contains the diffuse nebula NGC 7000 (the North America Nebula) and farther south the incomplete ring of the Veil Nebula, a supernova remnant. M27 in Vulpecula is a planetary.*

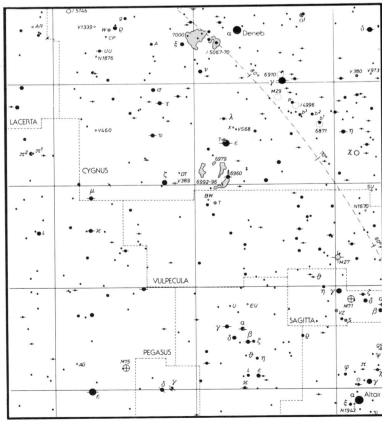

Part of the great Orion Nebula. Most of the light comes from glowing hydrogen gas, some of which is obscured by intervening dust, as on the left. The blue patch surrounding the star at right is a small reflection nebula.

Galaxies

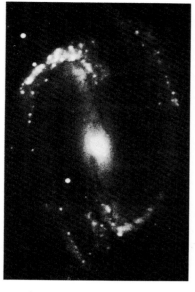

Above left *NGC 4569, an Sb galaxy, probably very similar to our own.*
Centre *the barred spiral (SBb) galaxy NGC 1300.* Above right *the edge-on
Sc spiral NGC 4565, showing a typical belt of dust.* Right *the E5 elliptical
galaxy NGC 205 that accompanies M31.*

Galaxies

Desig.	RA (2000) h	m	Dec. °	′	Type
M32	00	43	+40	53	E2
M31 (Great Andromeda Galaxy)	00	43	+41	17	Sb
SMC (Small Magellanic Cloud)	00	52	−73	14	Irr
M33	01	34	+30	39	Sc
LMC (Large Magellanic Cloud)	05	20	−69	00	Irr
M82	09	56	+59	42	Irr
M81	09	56	+69	04	Sb
M87	12	31	+12	23	EO
M104 (Sombrero)	12	40	−11	38	Sa/Sb
M94	12	51	+41	07	Sb
M64 (Black-Eye)	12	57	+21	41	Sa/Sb
NGC 5128	13	26	−43	00	S0/pec
M51 (Whirlpool)	13	30	+47	12	Sb
M83	13	37	−29	52	Sc
M101	14	03	+54	21	Sc

On a very clear night, the band of the Milky Way stretching around the sky and the suggestion of a bulge formed by the dense star clouds near Sagittarius give a hint of how the Galaxy consists of a disk and a central nucleus. The structure of external galaxies is easier to see. Some, such as M31, the Great Andromeda Galaxy and M33 in Triangulum, are spiral galaxies (S). These have wide, flat disks and long spiral arms of dust, gas and bright young stars. In the centre, their nuclei are flattened spheres of older, redder stars. (Our own galaxy is of this type.) Some spirals have arms that are widely spaced, but in others the arms are tightly wound around the nucleus. In a sub-class of spirals (the barred spirals, SB) the arms arise from the end of a distinct bar that runs across the centre.

The other major class is that of the elliptical galaxies. These are smooth balls of stars, some completely spherical (E0 galaxies), but others are more or less flattened by their rotation. The E7 galaxies show a long, thin ellipse when seen from the side. Somewhere between the ellipticals and the spirals come the S0 and SB0 galaxies, with central nuclei and smooth disks of stars. All elliptical galaxies have very little gas and dust, and their stars are old and red. The most massive galaxies of all are ellipticals, but others are very tiny, more like large globular clusters. M87, in Virgo, although it has certain peculiarities, is a giant E1 galaxy. M32 and NGC 205, the companions of the Andromeda Galaxy are smaller examples.

A final class consists of irregular galaxies. Not many of these are easily visible in small telescopes, but the Small Magellanic Cloud gives an indication of their appearance. (The Large Magellanic Cloud, long thought to be irregular, is now believed to have some spiral structure.) Bright blue stars are only found in spiral and irregular galaxies, the sign that only they are the sites of recent stellar formation.

External galaxies (like distant parts of our own Galaxy) are hidden by the dense clouds of stars and dust along the Milky Way. Most are therefore visible well away from the plane of the Galaxy, towards the galactic poles in Coma Berenices and Sculptor. The northern area (Coma, Leo and Virgo), in particular, is very rich in galaxies.

The nearest large galaxies M31 and M33 are visible to the naked eye, although the latter is a very difficult object to observe. M32 and NGC 205 (M110) are about magnitude 9, so always require a telescope to be seen.

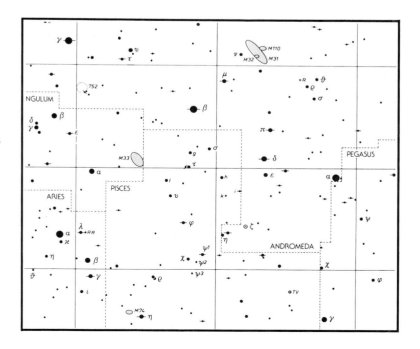

Northern hemisphere

0ʰ

CETUS

AQUARIUS

PISCES

Mira

EQUULEUS

PEGASUS

ARIES

ERIDANUS

4ʰ

20ʰ

4

DELPHINUS

TRIANGULUM

TAURUS

AQUILA

Altair

SAGITTA

LACERTA

ANDROMEDA

M 31

Pleiades

Hyades

Aldebaran

Rigel

VULPECULA

CYGNUS

Deneb

CASSIOPEIA

h χ

PERSEUS

Algol

M 42

ORION

SCUTUM

CEPHEUS

Capella

Betelgeuse

SERPENS CAUDA

LYRA

Vega

CAMELOPARDALIS

1

Polaris

AURIGA

M 35

DRACO

URSA MINOR

LYNX

Castor

Pollux

GEMINI

OPHIUCHUS

HERCULES

M 13

Procyon

CANIS MINOR

MONOCEROS

CORONA
BOREALIS

URSA MAJOR

M 44

CANCER

SERPENS CAPUT

CANES VENATICI

LEO MINOR

16ʰ

M 5

Arcturus

BOÖTES

COMA BERENICES

Regulus

LEO

HYDRA

8ʰ

LIBRA

VIRGO

AEQUATOR

SEXTANS

3

Epoch **2000.0**

ECLIPTICA

Spica

Wil Tirion

Stereographic projection

Mag. -1 0 1 2 3 4 5

12ʰ

Star Charts

The charts on these two pages show the whole of the sky and act as a key to the larger-scale charts on the following pages. The latter show stars down to magnitude six, which is about the limit for the naked eye under fairly good conditions. (A few bright, non-stellar objects such as clusters are shown on the charts above.)

The names of the constellations are the 88 Latin names recognized by the international Astronomical Union (listed on page 67). The standard abbreviations are sometimes used on the charts. The constellation boundaries are those finally established in 1930 after many years of confusion over the areas included in any particular constellation. The boundaries are all portions of lines of right ascension or circles of declination for 1875, so they give an indication of the amount of precession since that date.

The brightest stars have their own proper names, many of great antiquity, although a few – especially in the south – have been invented in recent times for the convenience of modern navigators. Within each constellation the bright stars were given Greek or Roman letter designations by Johannes Bayer in the first years of the seventeenth century. Usually, but not always, α is the brightest star, and the other letters follow in approximately descending order of brightness. Some

may carry supplementary numbers to help with identification, as for example in the series π^1 to π^6 in Orion. Bayer also employed Roman letters twice, the second time as capital letters, when he only reached letter Q. Capital letters from R onwards were used by Argelander in the middle of the nineteenth century to designate variable stars. Double Roman letters and numbers prefixed by 'V' were later found to be required to cope with all the variable stars that had been discovered. Bright novae are shown on these charts by a standard method of designation: the year of their eruption prefixed by the letter 'N' (e.g. N1901 in Perseus). Variable stars are shown on the charts if they reach (or once reached) magnitude 6 at maximum.

Non-stellar objects are named in various ways. Most of the brightest clusters and galaxies in the northern, and part of the southern, sky have Messier numbers (M1–M110). Objects shown on the charts with just numbers without a prefix (e.g. 7000, the North American Nebula in Cygnus) are NGC numbers from the *New General Catalogue of Nebulae and Clusters of Stars*, published by J.L.E. Dreyer in 1888, a revision of Sir John Herschel's earlier catalogue. Objects from Dreyer's later *Index Catalogues* (IC) are shown by the prefix 'I' (e.g. I·2602, the bright cluster including θ Carinae). Some notable objects are listed beside each pair of charts.

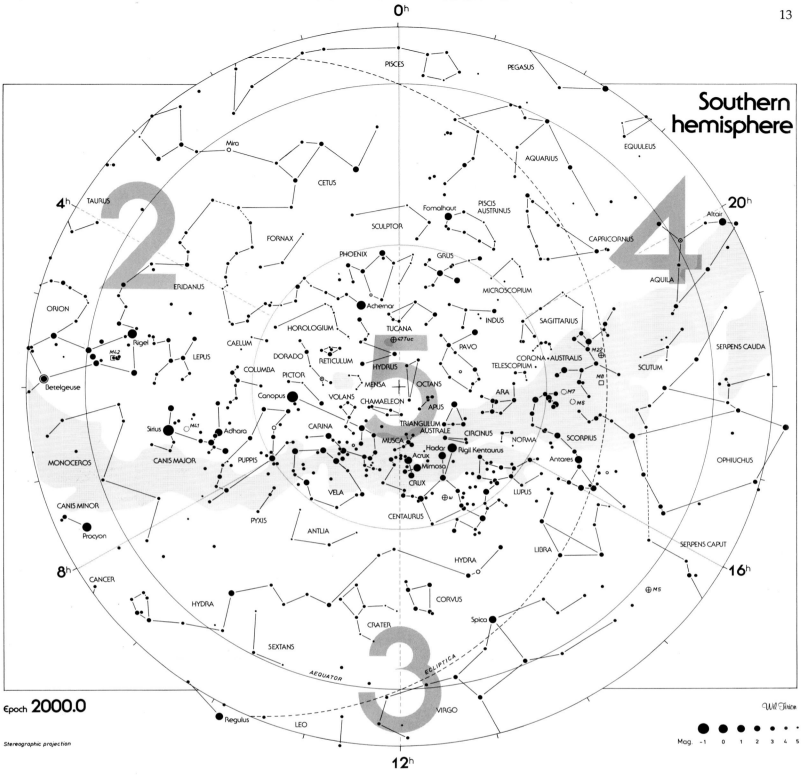

Southern hemisphere

Epoch **2000.0**

Stereographic projection

Wil Tirion

Mag. -1 0 1 2 3 4 5

The galactic equator (the central plane of the disk of the Galaxy) is shown, numbered in degrees where 0° indicates the direction of the galactic centre. The abbreviations NGP and SGP are used to mark the positions of the northern and southern galactic poles. The tinted area on the charts shows the most densely populated regions of the Milky Way. In the southern hemisphere the Large and Small Magellanic Clouds carry the abbreviations LMC and SMC.

The ecliptic is also shown, marked with ecliptic longitudes –

another form of co-ordinate system occasionally used – beginning at the vernal equinox. The Sun moves along the ecliptic at slightly less than 1° per day.

The visibility of particular regions depends upon the time of year, the time of day, and the observer's position on Earth. The table gives an approximate indication of when a particular hour of right ascension is on the meridian (and therefore best seen) at 00:00 hours (midnight) winter standard time. This applies to observers in both the northern and southern hemispheres. Objects with lesser RA (to the west) will be on the meridian before midnight, and those with greater RA after that time.

In theory, an observer at 40° north can see objects on the southern horizon at -50° declination. In practice, few objects can be observed within 10° of the horizon, so -40° is a more reasonable figure. Similarly for an observer in the southern hemisphere at -30° latitude, the 'working' horizon would be about +50° declination. The altitude of the pole in either hemisphere is the same as the latitude (disregarding the sign), and all objects less than that distance from the pole are circumpolar. Although objects within 10° of the horizon will still be obscured, they should become visible at some time during the night, although at high latitudes long summer twilight may prevent this from being the case.

Greek alphabet

upper case	lower case	name	upper case	lower case	name
A	α	alpha	N	ν	nu
B	β	beta	Ξ	ξ	xi
Γ	γ	gamma	O	o	omicron
Δ	δ	delta	Π	π	pi
E	ε	epsilon	P	ρ	rho
Z	ζ	zeta	Σ	σ	sigma
H	η	eta	T	τ	tau
Θ	θ	theta	Υ	υ	upsilon
I	ι	iota	Φ	φ	phi
K	κ	kappa	X	χ	chi
Λ	λ	lambda	Ψ	ψ	psi
M	μ	mu	Ω	ω	omega

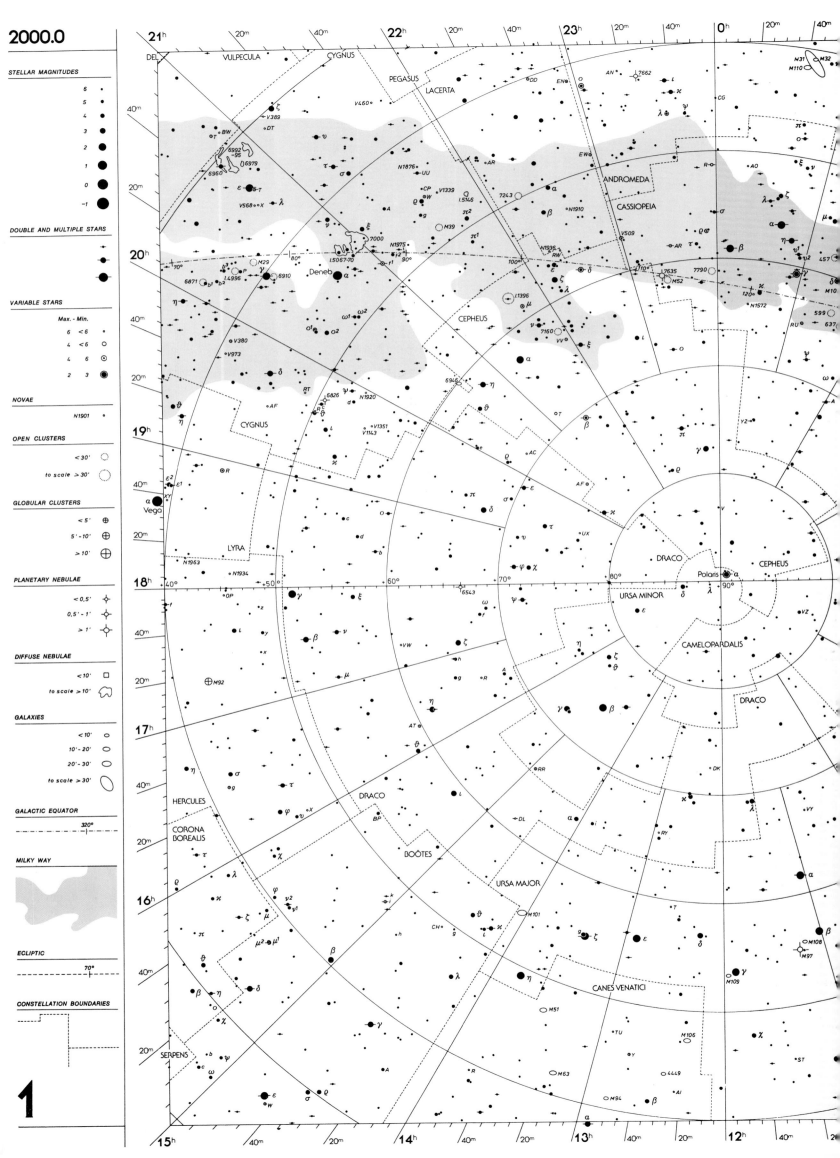

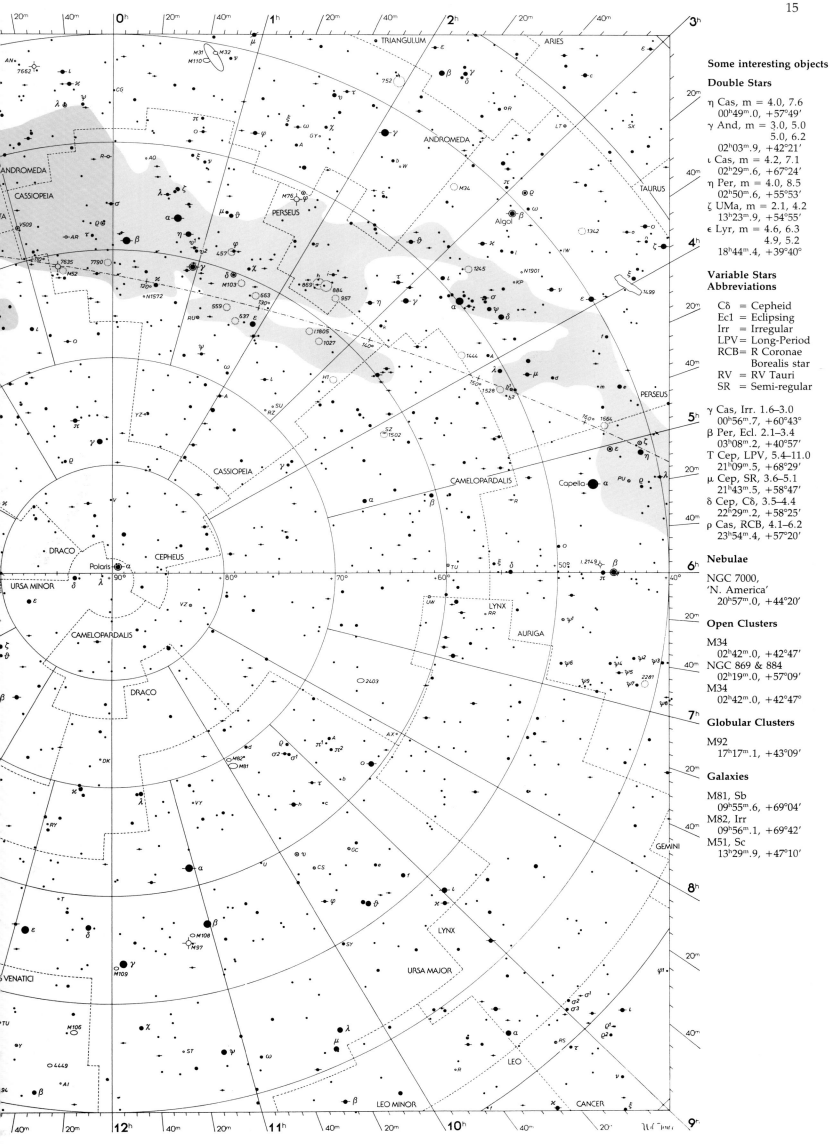

Some interesting objects

Double Stars

η Cas, m = 4.0, 7.6
  00ʰ49ᵐ.0, +57°49′
γ And, m = 3.0, 5.0
            5.0, 6.2
  02ʰ03ᵐ.9, +42°21′
ι Cas, m = 4.2, 7.1
  02ʰ29ᵐ.6, +67°24′
η Per, m = 4.0, 8.5
  02ʰ50ᵐ.6, +55°53′
ζ UMa, m = 2.1, 4.2
  13ʰ23ᵐ.9, +54°55′
ε Lyr, m = 4.6, 6.3
            4.9, 5.2
  18ʰ44ᵐ.4, +39°40°

Variable Stars
Abbreviations

Cδ = Cepheid
Ecl = Eclipsing
Irr = Irregular
LPV = Long-Period
RCB = R Coronae
        Borealis star
RV = RV Tauri
SR = Semi-regular

γ Cas, Irr. 1.6–3.0
  00ʰ56ᵐ.7, +60°43°
β Per, Ecl. 2.1–3.4
  03ʰ08ᵐ.2, +40°57′
T Cep, LPV, 5.4–11.0
  21ʰ09ᵐ.5, +68°29′
μ Cep, SR, 3.6–5.1
  21ʰ43ᵐ.5, +58°47′
δ Cep, Cδ, 3.5–4.4
  22ʰ29ᵐ.2, +58°25′
ρ Cas, RCB, 4.1–6.2
  23ʰ54ᵐ.4, +57°20′

Nebulae

NGC 7000,
'N. America'
  20ʰ57ᵐ.0, +44°20′

Open Clusters

M34
  02ʰ42ᵐ.0, +42°47′
NGC 869 & 884
  02ʰ19ᵐ.0, +57°09′
M34
  02ʰ42ᵐ.0, +42°47′

Globular Clusters

M92
  17ʰ17ᵐ.1, +43°09′

Galaxies

M81, Sb
  09ʰ55ᵐ.6, +69°04′
M82, Irr
  09ʰ56ᵐ.1, +69°42′
M51, Sc
  13ʰ29ᵐ.9, +47°10′

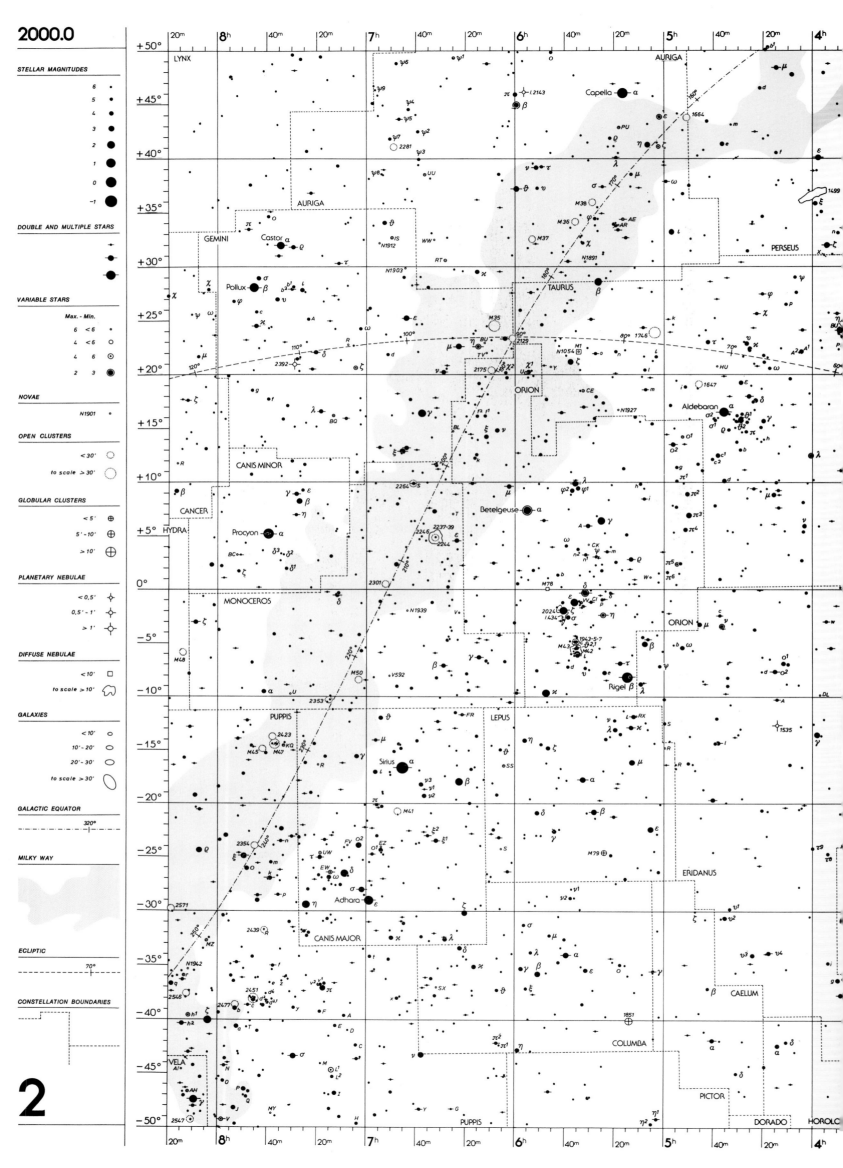

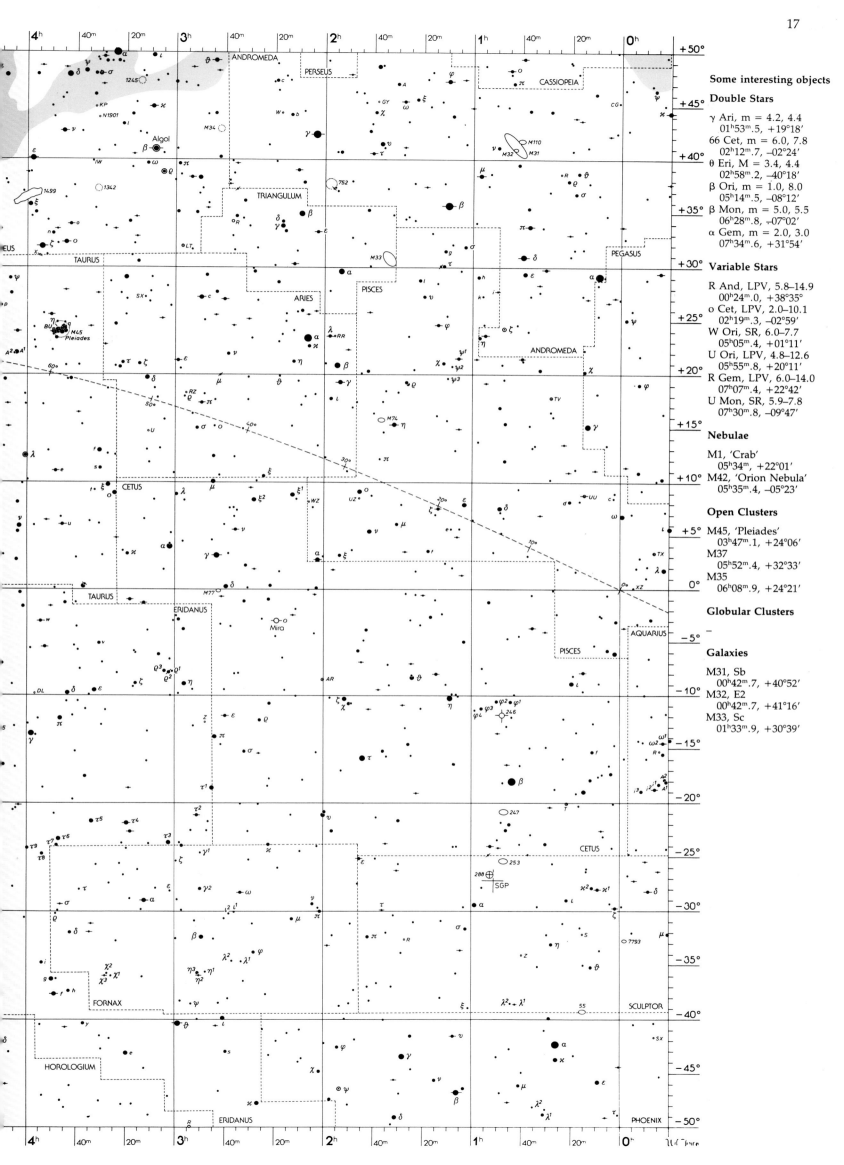

Some interesting objects

Double Stars

γ Ari, m = 4.2, 4.4
  01h53m.5, +19°18′
66 Cet, m = 6.0, 7.8
  02h12m.7, −02°24′
θ Eri, M = 3.4, 4.4
  02h58m.2, −40°18′
β Ori, m = 1.0, 8.0
  05h14m.5, −08°12′
β Mon, m = 5.0, 5.5
  06h28m.8, −07°02′
α Gem, m = 2.0, 3.0
  07h34m.6, +31°54′

Variable Stars

R And, LPV, 5.8–14.9
  00h24m.0, +38°35′
o Cet, LPV, 2.0–10.1
  02h19m.3, −02°59′
W Ori, SR, 6.0–7.7
  05h05m.4, +01°11′
U Ori, LPV, 4.8–12.6
  05h55m.8, +20°11′
R Gem, LPV, 6.0–14.0
  07h07m.4, +22°42′
U Mon, SR, 5.9–7.8
  07h30m.8, −09°47′

Nebulae

M1, 'Crab'
  05h34m, +22°01′
M42, 'Orion Nebula'
  05h35m.4, −05°23′

Open Clusters

M45, 'Pleiades'
  03h47m.1, +24°06′
M37
  05h52m.4, +32°33′
M35
  06h08m.9, +24°21′

Globular Clusters

–

Galaxies

M31, Sb
  00h42m.7, +40°52′
M32, E2
  00h42m.7, +41°16′
M33, Sc
  01h33m.9, +30°39′

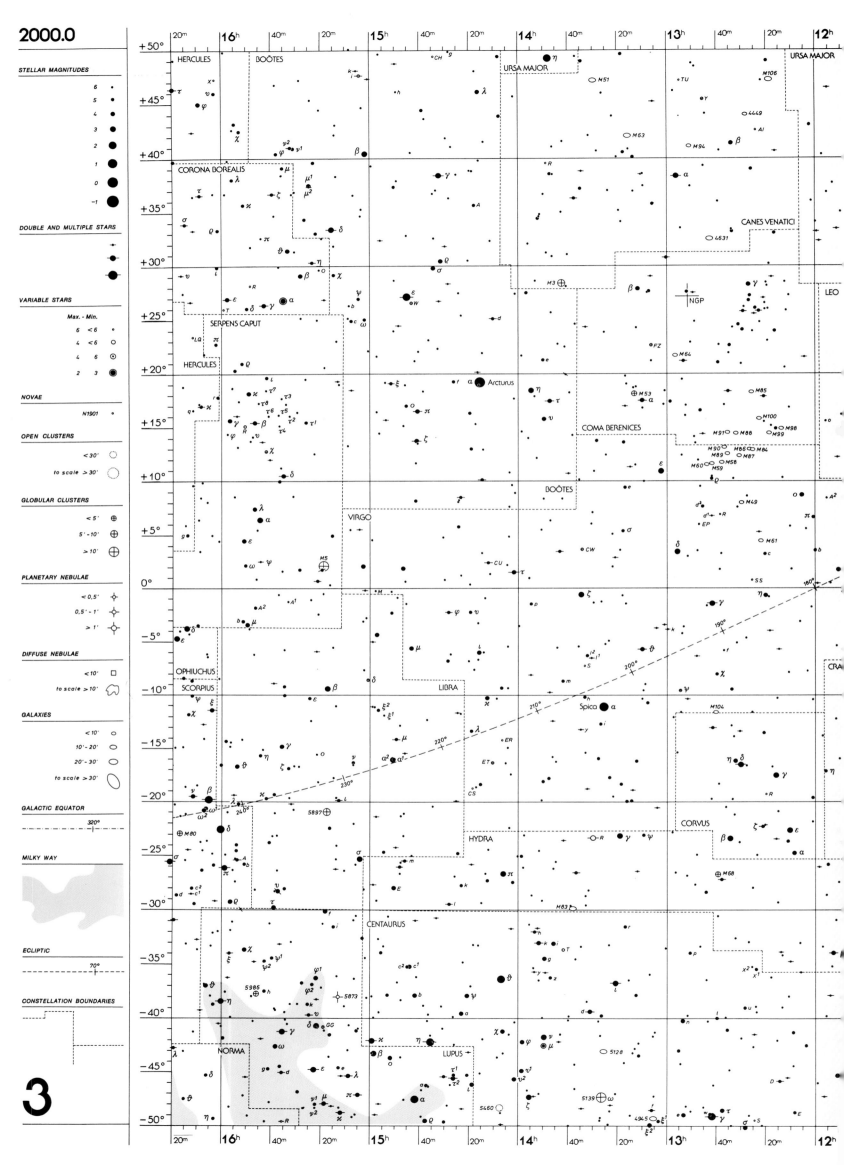

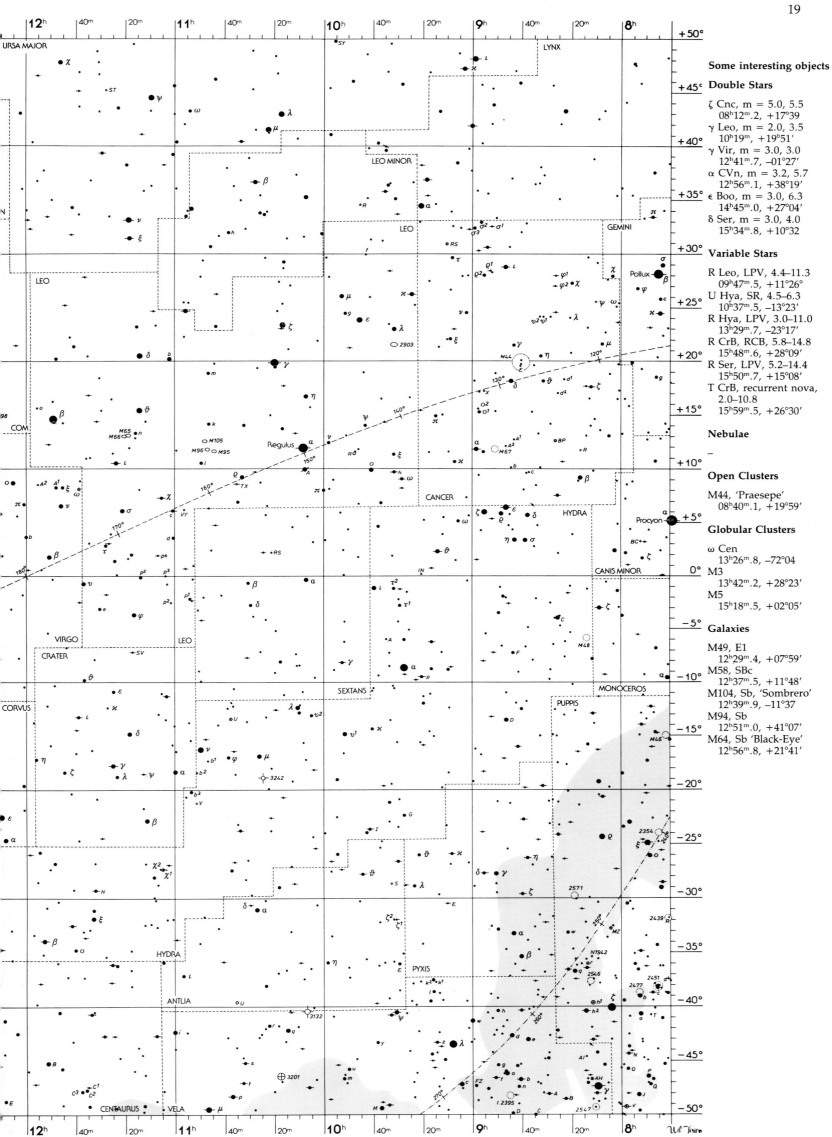

Some interesting objects

Double Stars

ζ Cnc, m = 5.0, 5.5
  $08^h12^m.2$, +17°39
γ Leo, m = 2.0, 3.5
  10^h19^m, +19°51'
γ Vir, m = 3.0, 3.0
  $12^h41^m.7$, −01°27'
α CVn, m = 3.2, 5.7
  $12^h56^m.1$, +38°19'
ε Boo, m = 3.0, 6.3
  $14^h45^m.0$, +27°04'
δ Ser, m = 3.0, 4.0
  $15^h34^m.8$, +10°32

Variable Stars

R Leo, LPV, 4.4–11.3
  $09^h47^m.5$, +11°26°
U Hya, SR, 4.5–6.3
  $10^h37^m.5$, −13°23'
R Hya, LPV, 3.0–11.0
  $13^h29^m.7$, −23°17'
R CrB, RCB, 5.8–14.8
  $15^h48^m.6$, +28°09'
R Ser, LPV, 5.2–14.4
  $15^h50^m.7$, +15°08'
T CrB, recurrent nova,
  2.0–10.8
  $15^h59^m.5$, +26°30'

Nebulae

—

Open Clusters

M44, 'Praesepe'
  $08^h40^m.1$, +19°59'

Globular Clusters

ω Cen
  $13^h26^m.8$, −72°04
M3
  $13^h42^m.2$, +28°23'
M5
  $15^h18^m.5$, +02°05'

Galaxies

M49, E1
  $12^h29^m.4$, +07°59'
M58, SBc
  $12^h37^m.5$, +11°48'
M104, Sb, 'Sombrero'
  $12^h39^m.9$, −11°37
M94, Sb
  $12^h51^m.0$, +41°07'
M64, Sb 'Black-Eye'
  $12^h56^m.8$, +21°41'

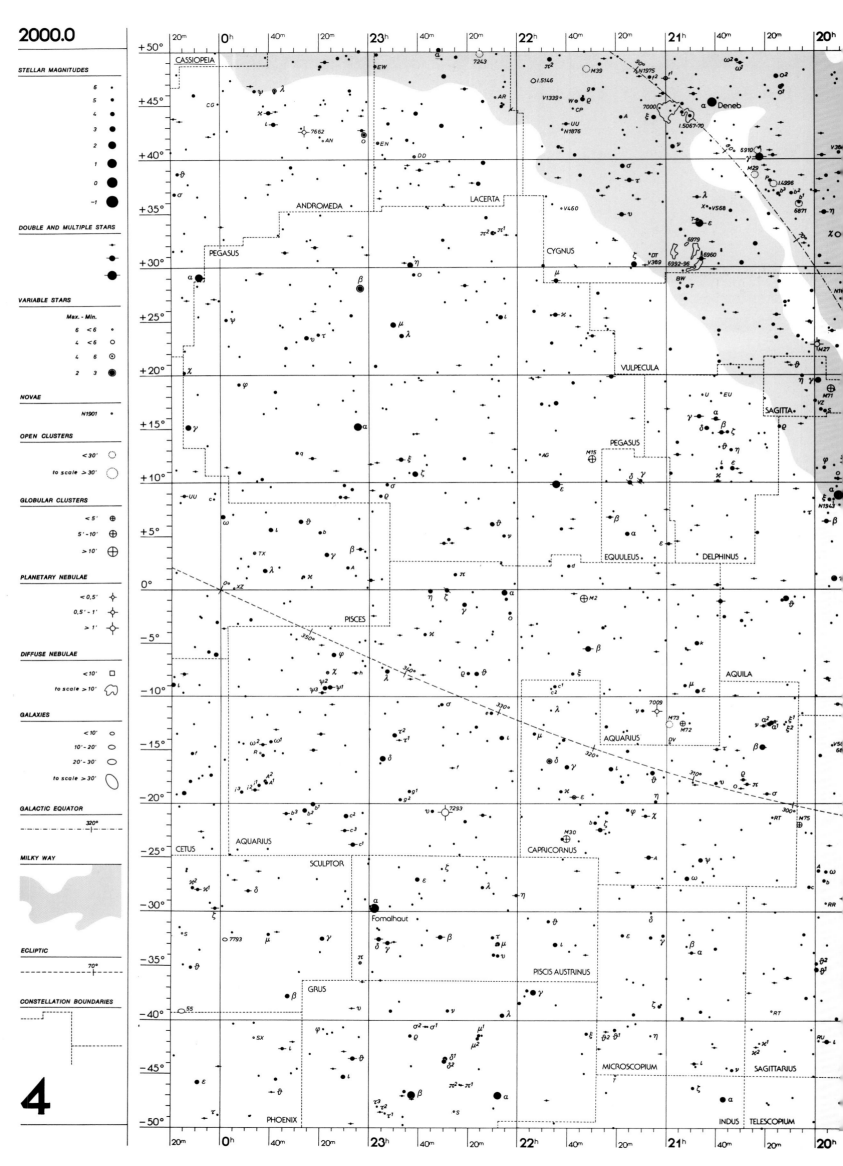

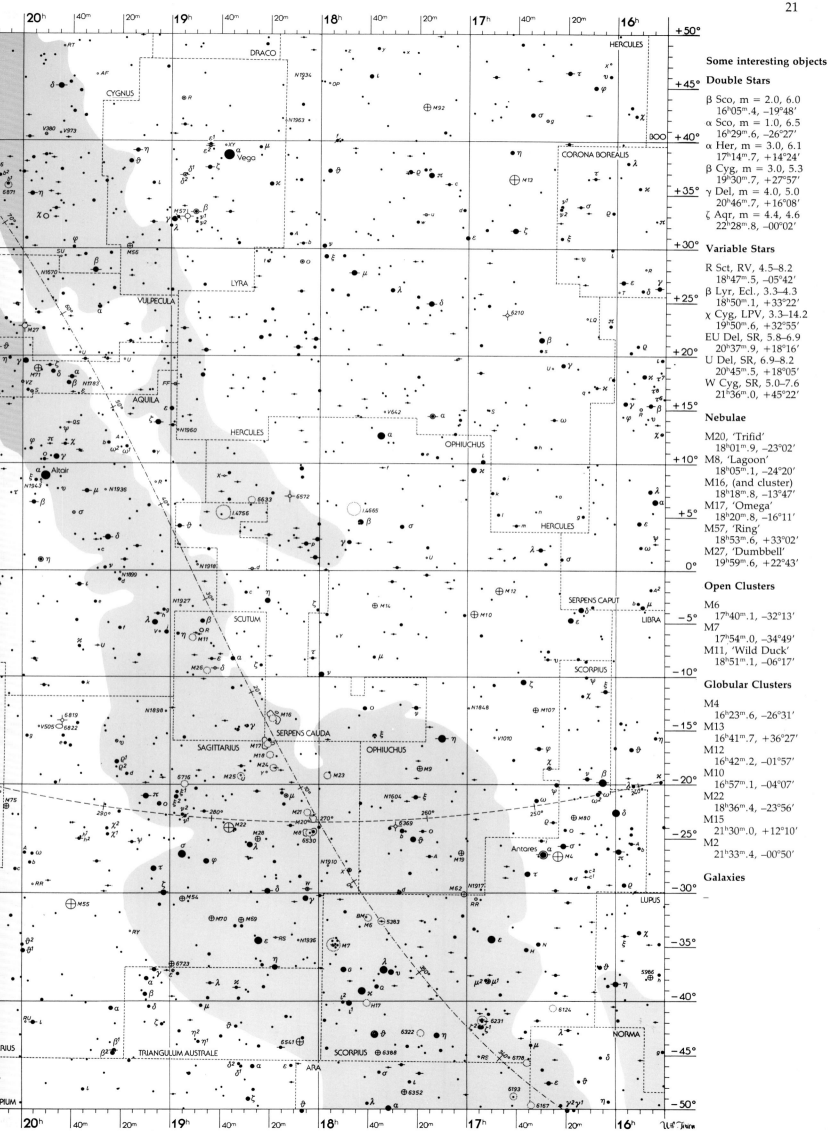

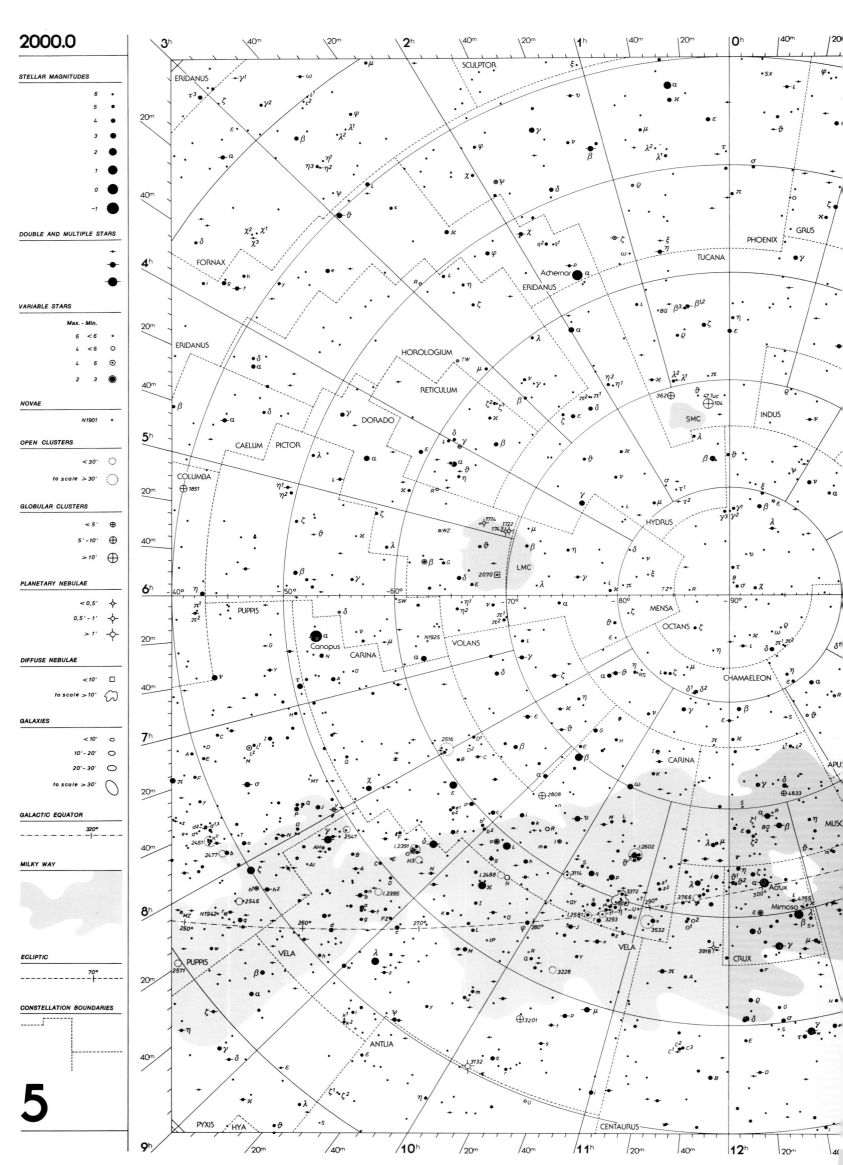

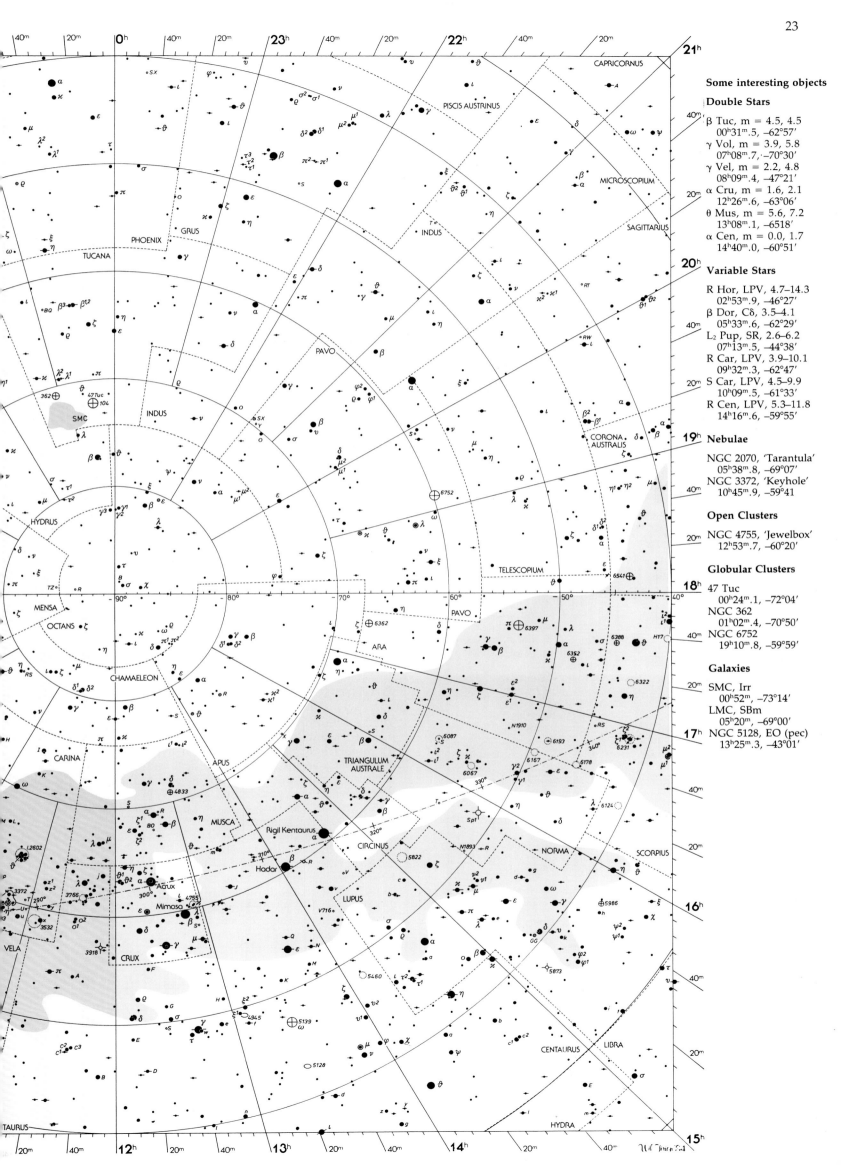

Some interesting objects

Double Stars

β Tuc, m = 4.5, 4.5
00h31m.5, −62°57′
γ Vol, m = 3.9, 5.8
07h08m.7, −70°30′
γ Vel, m = 2.2, 4.8
08h09m.4, −47°21′
α Cru, m = 1.6, 2.1
12h26m.6, −63°06′
θ Mus, m = 5.6, 7.2
13h08m.1, −6518′
α Cen, m = 0.0, 1.7
14h40m.0, −60°51′

Variable Stars

R Hor, LPV, 4.7–14.3
02h53m.9, −46°27′
β Dor, Cδ, 3.5–4.1
05h33m.6, −62°29′
L₂ Pup, SR, 2.6–6.2
07h13m.5, −44°38′
R Car, LPV, 3.9–10.1
09h32m.3, −62°47′
S Car, LPV, 4.5–9.9
10h09m.5, −61°33′
R Cen, LPV, 5.3–11.8
14h16m.6, −59°55′

Nebulae

NGC 2070, 'Tarantula'
05h38m.8, −69°07′
NGC 3372, 'Keyhole'
10h45m.9, −59°41

Open Clusters

NGC 4755, 'Jewelbox'
12h53m.7, −60°20′

Globular Clusters

47 Tuc
00h24m.1, −72°04′
NGC 362
01h02m.4, −70°50′
NGC 6752
19h10m.8, −59°59′

Galaxies

SMC, Irr
00h52m, −73°14′
LMC, SBm
05h20m, −69°00′
NGC 5128, EO (pec)
13h25m.3, −43°01′

Constellation maps

Constellations: Introduction

Individual charts of the 88 constellations are shown on this and the following pages, together with brief details concerning some of the most notable objects in each region. The headings give the official names, followed by the Latin genitives, the standard three-letter abbreviations, and (where applicable) the usual translations.

The constellations differ very widely in size, ranging from the large Virgo (1294 square degrees) down to Crux (68 square degrees). The constellation of Hydra covers nearly 7 hours in right ascension, and Eridanus nearly 60° in declination. Because of these differences in size, the most appropriate scale has been chosen for each constellation. The celestial co-ordinate grid is shown in black, with markings every hour in right ascension and 10° in declination. One of the lines of right ascension carries an arrow indicating North, which is usually towards the top of the page. The region of sky covered by each constellation is shown by the blue tint.

Individual stars are identified on these charts down to magnitude 5. For the fainter stars the designations are the Flamsteed numbers, originally assigned by Flamsteed, the first English Astronomer Royal in 1725. These stars were listed in increasing right ascension within each constellation. When the constellation boundaries were settled in 1930, some of the fainter Flamsteed stars came outside their original constellations, in a neighbouring area. To prevent confusion they retain their old names. An example is 10 UMa, now in Lynx.

Asterisms are striking groups of stars that may form part of one or more constellations. These are often useful for identification and some of the best-known are listed here, together with some pairs of stars with individual names.

Asterisms

Name	Stars
Belt of Orion	δ, ε, and ζ Orionis
Big Dipper	α, β, γ, δ, 3, ζ, and η Ursae Majoris
Bull of Poniatowski	66, 67, 68, and 70 Ophiuchi
Circlet	γ, b, θ, ι, 19, λ, and κ Piscium
False Cross	ε and ι Carinae δ and κ Velorum
Frederick's Glory	ι, κ, λ, and ψ Andromedae
Guards (or Guardians)	β and γ Ursa Minoris
Head of Cetus	α, γ, ζ₂, μ, and λ Ceti
Head of Draco	β, γ, ξ, and ω Draconis
Head of Hydra	δ, ε, ζ, η,ρ, and σ Hydrae
Keystone	ε, ζ, η, and π Herculis
Kids	ε, ζ, and η Aurigae
Little Dipper	β, γ, ς, ζ, ε, δ, and α Ursae Minoris
Lozenge	Head of Draco
Milk Dipper	ζ, γ, σ, φ, and λ Sagittarii
Pointers	α and β Ursae Majoris
Sickle	ζ, η, γ, ζ,η, and σ Leonis
Square of Pegasus	α, β, and γ Pegasi and α Andromedae
Sword of Orion	θ and ι Orionis
Teapot	γ, ε, δ, λ, φ, σ, τ, and ζ Sagittarii
Wain	as Big Dipper
Water Jar	γ, η, κ, and ζ Aquarii

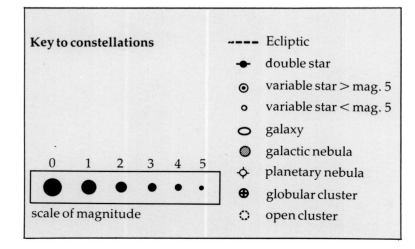

Key to constellations
scale of magnitude
0 1 2 3 4 5

Andromeda

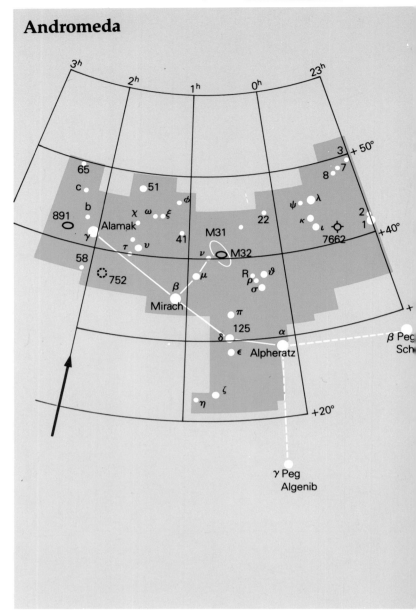

Andromeda Andromedae And *Andromeda*

This is one of the oldest named constellations and formed part of Ptolemy's catalogue of the second century AD. Mythological legend surrounds the story of the naming of Andromeda and it is one of the best-known groups in the sky, not so much perhaps for the stars it contains but because it includes M31, a giant spiral galaxy very close to our own. These two are the largest in the Local Group of galaxies which contains about 20 members.

The three most prominent stars are laid out along Dec 30–40 and virtually span the constellation. Star β, Mirach, is a mag 2·02 M0 type with absolute mag 0·2, lying at a distance of 76 light years. Originally in the constellation of Pegasus, and indeed right on the border, can be found α, Alpheratz, a mag 2·06 B9 star with absolute mag −0·1, 90 light years from the Solar System. In the opposite direction towards Perseus, γ, Almaak is a mag 2·14 K3 type with absolute mag −2·4 some 260 light years distant. It is actually a multiple star with components of mag 3·0, 5·0, 5·0 and 6·2.

Heading almost directly north from star δ, the keen observer will see with the naked eye a faint hazy patch lying on a similar declination to Almaak. This is the Great Andromeda Galaxy, M31, which has a total magnitude of 5·0. The galaxy is about $2·2 \times 10^6$ light years away.

- - - - Ecliptic
● double star
◉ variable star > mag. 5
○ variable star < mag. 5
⬭ galaxy
◍ galactic nebula
◇ planetary nebula
⊕ globular cluster
⦂ open cluster

Antlia

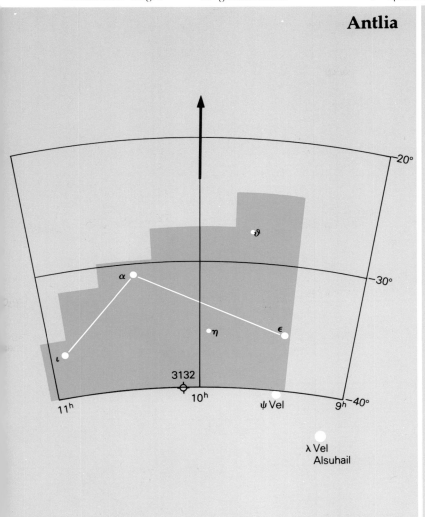

Apus

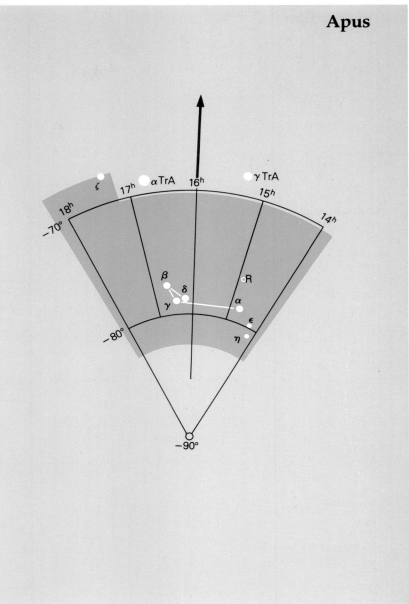

Antlia Antliae Ant *Pump*

This is a southern sky constellation flanked by Centaurus, Hydra, Pyxis and Vela, which is inconspicuous and comparatively unimportant for object content or direction seeking.

Apus Apodis Aps *Bird of Paradise*

Apus is another southern sky constellation which was added by Bayer in the 17th century. It was originally known as Apus Indica. Apus is flanked by the constellations Musca, Chamaeleon, Octans, Pavo, Ara, Triangulum Australe and Circinus. No interesting stars are contained in this group and the most prominent is the mag 3·8 α. θ is an irregular variable of class M and varies between mag 5·0 and 6·6.

Aquarius

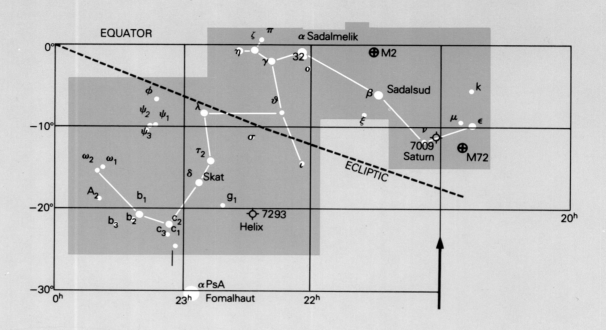

Aquarius Aquarii Aqr *Water Bearer*

Aquarius is one of the 12 constellations of the zodiac, and one of the oldest named groups. The mythological representation of a water-bearer influenced the Egyptians to believe that its ascendant appearance over the horizon with the Sun brought fertility to the land.

The constellation is flanked by Pegasus, Equuleus, Delphinus, Aquila, Capricornus, Piscis Austrinus, Sculptor, Cetus and Pisces. It extends from RA 20 hr 35 min–23 hr 55 min and from Dec 3 −25, a sprawling expanse of the ecliptic plane. The brightest star in the group is β, Sadalsud, of visual mag 2·86 and absolute mag −4·6, which is very similar to the Sun in class but a supergiant by type. Star α, called Sadalmelik, is of mag 2·96 and from here a triangle of stars can be seen representing the jug carried by the mythological water-bearer. The constellation also contains the Saturn Nebula named because of its similarity to the ringed planet, and the famous Helix Nebula, NGC 7293.

Aquila Aquilae Aql *Eagle*

This is a prominent summer constellation named after the mythological eagle sent to carry Ganymedes to Olympus. Aquila has consistently been associated with birds and the triangular outline is seen to represent a bird with outstretched wings.

Lying generally in the direction of the Milky Way, Aquila is sometimes difficult to pick out from the star clouds beyond. Star α, Altair, is a very bright white star to the east of the apex, only 16 light years from Earth, and is an A7 class source of mag 0·77 (absolute mag 2·2). It is flanked by Tarazed γ Aquilae, 340 light years away (mag 2·7) and Alshain β (mag 3·9). Star η Aquilae is a prominent Cepheid variable (mag 3·7–4·4) with a period of seven days.

Aquila

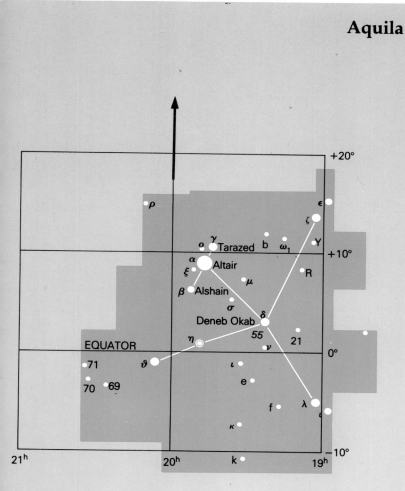

Ara

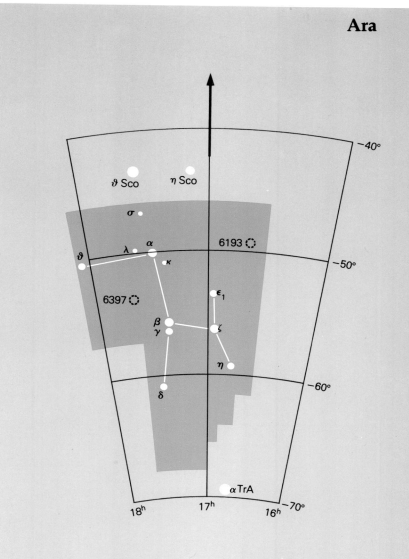

Ara *Arae Ara Altar*

Ara has precessed considerably from the position it held when named. It lies far to the south but was visible from the Mediterranean in 1000 BC and was so named because of its apparent similarity to an altar.

Ara is a mediocre collection of stars with members β and α of mag 2·9 and spectral types K3 and B2 respectively (absolute mags are −4·3 and −2·4 due to the 1030 and 390 light year distance).

Aries

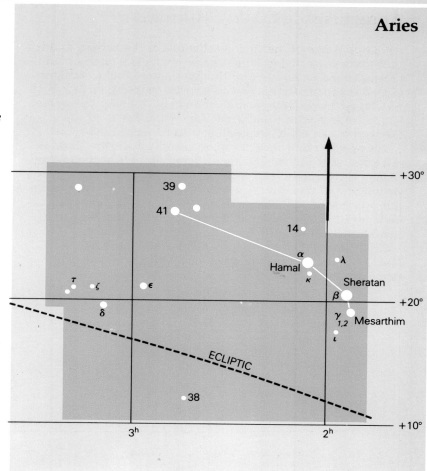

Aries *Arietis Ari Ram*

Aries, named by the Greeks after the ram with the Golden Fleece, bequeathed its name to the zero point of the system of RA, because the vernal equinox was once located in the constellation. Precession has shifted the equinox into Pisces which, together with Triangulum, Perseus, Taurus and Cetus, borders the constellation.

Aries has only two stars above magnitude 4. These are α, Hamal, with mag 2·0 (76 light years distant) and β, Sheratan, of mag 2·7 (52 light years distant) of spectral types K2 and A5 respectively. The third named star, γ, Mesartim, is double with mags 4·2 and 4·4. Its name may come from the Arabic word for 'The Sign' and refers to the alignment with the vernal equinox in early history.

Auriga

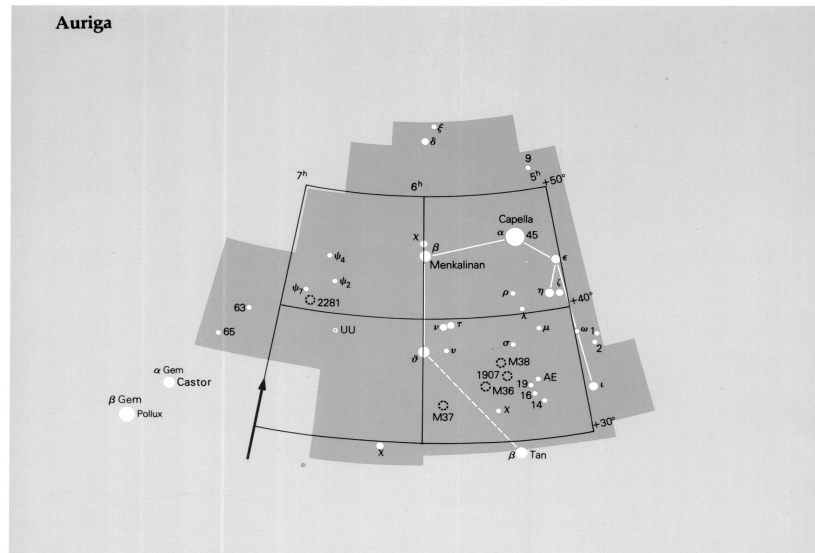

Auriga Aurigae Aur *Charioteer*

Although it is accepted that Auriga represents a bearded man carrying a goat, the Assyrians viewed this as a chariot and the Greeks saw it as a lame man riding a horse. Auriga achieves fame today from the star ε Aurigae, an eclipsing binary (with 27-year period) with a mag 3 component, orbiting the largest star yet observed – an infrared body some $3 \cdot 0 \times 10^9$ km across, both of which lie 3400 light years from Earth.

The brighter component can be seen through the tenuous envelope of the larger star, and therefore the system appears to be a single variable. ζ Aurigae is an eclipsing binary with a period of 3 years, and the star α, Capella, is interesting since it is a bright (mag 0·05) spectroscopic binary 45 light years away. It has components of 4·3 and 3·3 solar masses and a period of 104 days.

Other prominent stars are β, Menkalinan, an A2 type of mag 1·86, ι of K3 type and mag 2·64 and θ a B9 star of mag 2·65.

Caelum

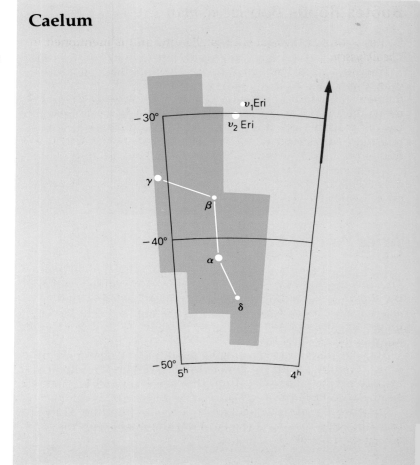

Ecliptic — — — —
double star
variable star > mag. 5

variable star < mag. 5
galaxy
galactic nebula

planetary nebula
globular cluster
open cluster

Boötes

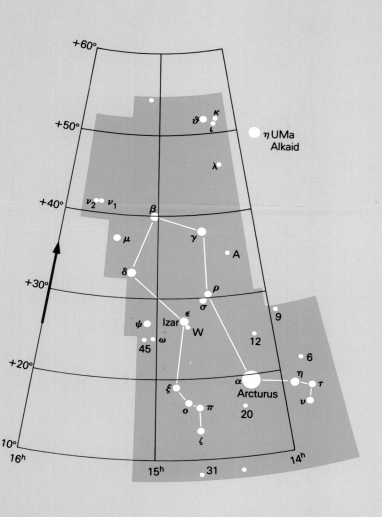

Camelopardalis

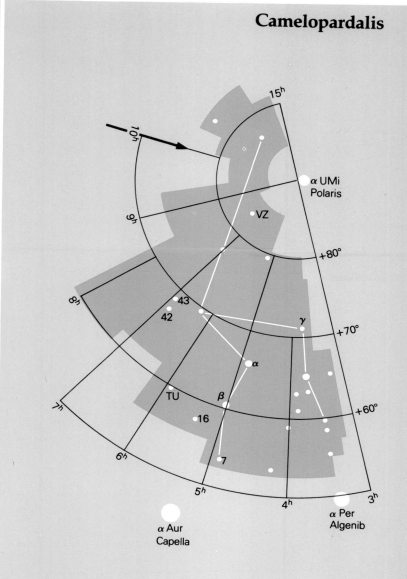

Boötes Boötis Boo *Herdsman*

Boötes is one of the oldest constellations and is mentioned in *The Odyssey*.

The most important star is α, Arcturus, of mag −0·06, an orange giant K2 type 40 light years away and 30 times the diameter of the Sun. Arcturus was one of the stars first measured by Halley to have motion relative to the Sun. ε, Izar, of mag 3·0, is a double star (companion mag 6·3) often referred to as one of the most beautiful stars in the sky, and frequently given the name Pulcherrima, 'Most Beautiful'.

Other visible elements in the constellation are η, Saak, of mag 2·69, and γ, Seginus, of mag 3·0, 32 and 118 light years away respectively.

Caelum Caeli Cae *Chisel*

This inconspicuous southern constellation is best dedicated to the memory of the little known astronomer Lacaille than to any serious observational activity. Lacaille studied at the Paris Observatory and made major contributions to establishing an accurate measure of the arc of the meridian. Later, from 1751–3, he derived the positions of some 10 000 stars during which time he set up the constellation Caelum. No other astronomer has made a greater contribution to the mapping of southern constellations.

For northern observers Caelum is a winter group and can be easily seen only south of latitude 30°N. It has no objects of any great interest.

Camelopardalis Camelopardalis Cam *Giraffe*

This is an inconspicuous constellation occupying a fairly large region of the northern circumpolar sky. Its name, first used by Bartschius in 1614 but believed to have been derived earlier, has been variously given as Camelopardus and Camelopardis.

The constellation occupies a relatively barren region of space and the seven brightest stars are all between mag 4–5. This constellation contains little of interest among the bright objects, although some variable stars are visible with binoculars. Its boundaries are very irregular, especially the western one, which meanders towards Ursa Minor with numerous changes of direction.

Constellation maps

Cancer

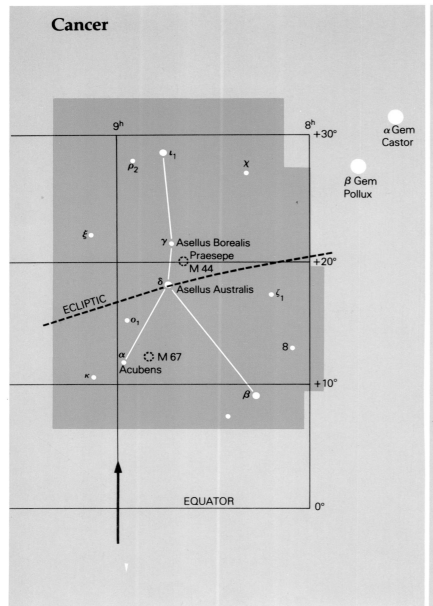

Canis Major

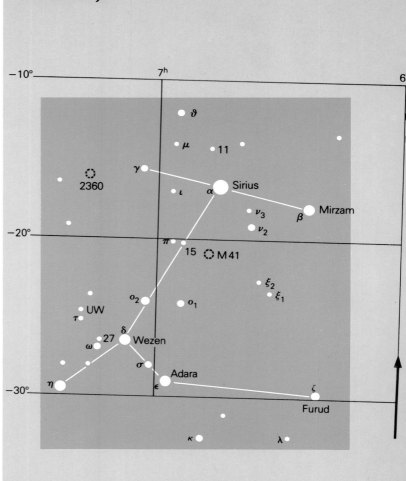

Cancer Cancri Cnc *Crab*

Cancer is an old constellation and one of the 12 zodiacal groups. Several thousand years ago this constellation formed the background to the Sun when the latter reached the summer solstice, its maximum elevation above the celestial equator (23·5°). The Sun was directly overhead along latitude 23·5°N and this line around the Earth was known as the Tropic of Cancer. Precession has now displaced this constellation from the solstice, which now lies on the border of Gemini and Cancer. Cancer contains no stars greater than 4th mag and the only interesting objects are two open clusters, M44 and M67. M44 is displaced from a line joining stars γ and δ centred on Dec 20 and contains more than 300 stars between mags 6 and 12, a group known as Praesepe.

Canes Venatici Canum Venaticorum CVn *Hunting Dogs*

Canes Venatici was set up in the late 17th century to fill a gap in Ptolemy's original 48 constellations. It is flanked by Ursa Major, Coma Berenice and Boötes. The only bright star is α, Cor Caroli, a mag 3·2 A0 type, 91 light years from Earth.

The constellation contains four interesting objects other than Cor Caroli. A globular cluster, M3, is located on the extreme southern boundary of the constellation. It contains over 10^5 stars in a sphere 65 light years across, 6×10^4 light years away. M51, close to the north-west boundary, is the famous Whirlpool Nebula, a spiral galaxy. M63, north-east of Cor Caroli, is another spiral galaxy (mag 9·6) as is NGC 4258 (mag 9·2) north-east of star β.

Canes Venatici

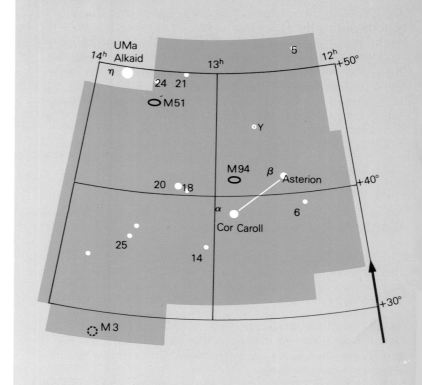

---- Ecliptic
○ variable star < mag. 5   ◇ planetary nebula
● double star
○ galaxy   ⊕ globular cluster
◉ variable star > mag. 5   ◉ galactic nebula   ○ open cluster

Canis Minor

Capricornus

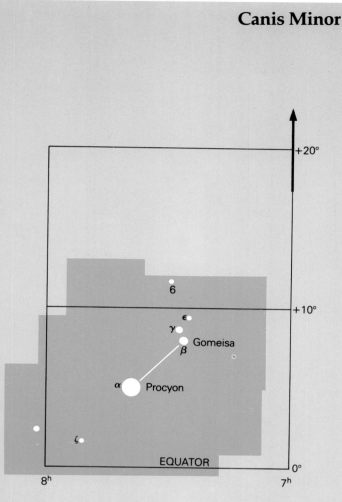

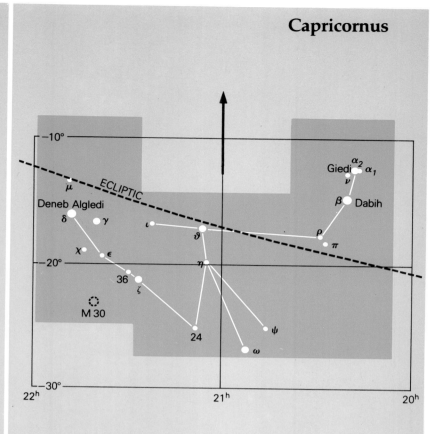

Canis Major Canis Majoris CMa *Big Dog*

The most important star in this constellation is α Canis Majoris, Sirius the Dog star, so named because it is the brightest component of Canis Major which, to the Egyptians, represented Anubis, the jackal-headed god. Sirius rose just before the Sun when the Nile was about to begin its yearly flood, and therefore was of great importance in the Egyptian calendar.

Sirius is a mag −1·43 A1 type less than 9 light years away and is the brightest star in the sky. It is accompanied by a faint companion orbiting 2.9×10^9 km away in 49·9 years (mag 9.1). Sirius B was the first white dwarf to be discovered. Canis Major contains four other stars brighter than mag 2·5 and also, M41, an open cluster 1300 light years away. Many of the stars are in fact intrinsically brighter than Sirius but at very great distances, rendering them visually fainter than this nearby star.

Capricornus Capricorni Cap *Sea Goat*

This constellation was associated with the lowest point reached by the Sun below the celestial equator (23·5°) at winter solstice for northern observers. It therefore gave its name to the Tropic of Capricorn for latitude 23.5° S.

The main star, δ, Deneb Algedi, is a mag 2·95–2·88 variable A6 type about 50 light years distant. Two naked-eye doubles are of interest: α, Prima Giedi, is of mag 3·2 with a binary companion of mag 9, and Secunda Giedi, is mag 3·8 with a binary companion of mag 11. The second pair, β, Dabih, is very close with mags 3·3 and 6. A globular cluster, M30, lies below Deneb Algedi.

Canis Minor Canis Minoris CMi *Little Dog*

Canis Minor is bounded on two sides by Monoceros and contains two stars of interest. Procyon, a mag 0·37 F5 star 11·5 light years distant, and β, Gomeisa, of mag 2·9 but of luminosity −1·1 due to its 210 light year distance. Procyon is six times solar luminosity, twice the size of the Sun but only 1·1 times the mass. Procyon and Gomeisa are the only two prominent objects in the constellation.

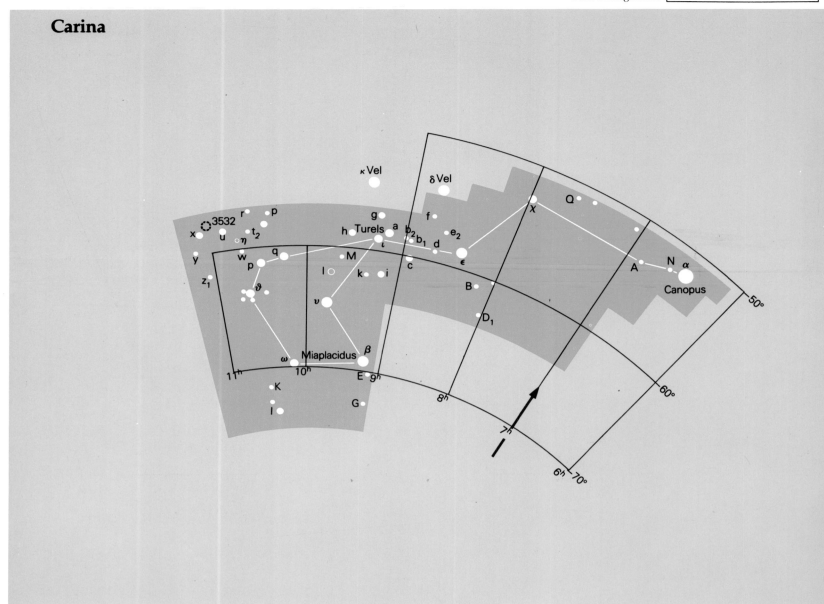

Carina Carinae Car *Keel (of a ship)*

Once part of the great sprawling Argo Navis, Carina is now separated (as are Puppis and Vela) and occupies a large portion of the southern sky. The constellation contains the second brightest star in the sky – Canopus, used by planetary spacecraft as a reference point for navigation.

Canopus is mag −0·73, and an F0 type star with an absolute mag of + 1·4. Other companions are β, Miaplacidus, a mag 1·67 A0 type 86 light years away, ε Carinae, a mag 1·97 K0 type at a distance of 340 light years and ι, Tureis, a 2·25 mag F0 star 750 light years distant. A rich globular cluster, NGC 2808, lies due east of v, a mag 2·97 A7 star. An interesting variable, η Carinae, grew from mag 4 to rival Sirius by 1843 and then, 10 years later, dimmed to its current mag 8.

Cassiopeia Cassiopeiae Cas *Cassiopeia*

Two of the main stars in Cassiopeia, α, Schedir, and γ, Tsih, are variable (about mag 2·16 and 1·6–2·9, respectively). The latter has a mag 8·18 companion. Of the remaining three stars making up the famous 'W' β, Caph, is a mag 2·26 F2 type, δ, Ruchbah, is a mag 2·67 A5 (probably an eclipsing variable with a 759-day period) and ε Cassiopeiae, is mag 3·3.

All but the last are less than 150 light years distant but ε is 500 light years away with an absolute mag of −2·7. The southern half of the constellation contains part of the Milky Way and many open clusters populate the region including M52 and M103. Cassiopeia lies opposite Ursa Major across the celestial north pole.

Centaurus Centauri Cen *Centaur*

Centaurus is a large constellation containing many bright stars, particulary the striking pair α and β Centauri. The α Centauri system is interesting as it is the closest binary to the Sun and has components of magnitudes 0·01 and 1·7. A further faint (mag 11) star, known as Proxima Centauri, is believed to orbit the bright pair. It is the closest star to the Solar System and lies at a distance of about 4·3 light years. The other bright star, β Cen, Hadar, is 390 light years away and has an absolute magnitude of −5·2.

Centaurus, containing part of the Milky Way, is a fine region to study with binoculars. A bright globular cluster, ω Cen, is easily located by prolonging the line from β to ε Cen. Its actual distance is about 17,000 light years.

Cepheus Cephei Cep *Cepheus*

This constellation contains δ Cephei, the prototype Cepheid variable with a mag of 3·51 – 4·42 and a period of 5·4 days. α, Alderamin, is an A7 2·44 mag star 52 light years away and β, Alphirk, is a variable (mag 3·14–3·19) binary. The only other bright stars of note are γ, Er Rai, a mag 3·2 object, ζ Cephei (mag 3·31) and μ, the 'Garnet Star', which appears a deep red colour.

- - - - Ecliptic
- ◆ double star
- ⊙ variable star > mag. 5
- ○ variable star < mag. 5
- ⬭ galaxy
- ⬤ galactic nebula
- ◇ planetary nebula
- ⊕ globular cluster
- ⚪ open cluster

Cassiopeia

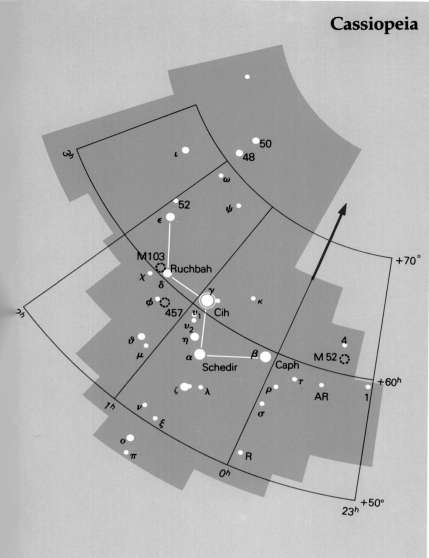

Cepheus

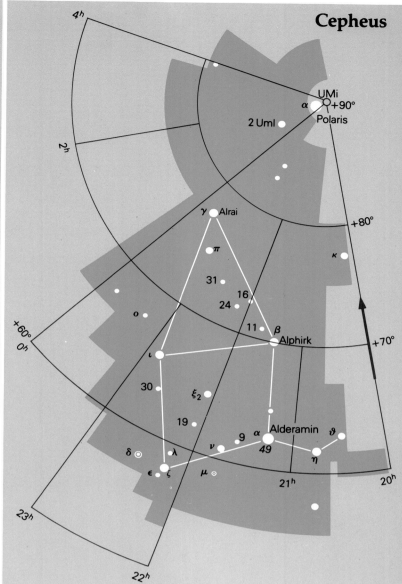

Centaurus

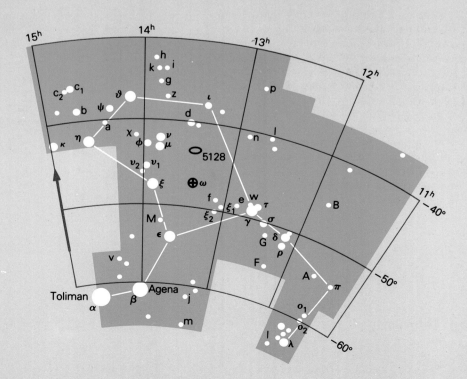

Cetus

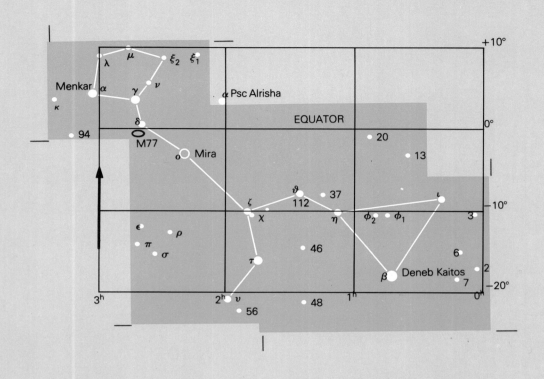

Cetus Ceti Cet *Whale*

The most famous object in Cetus is a striking variable star. Known as Mira, the star *o* Ceti is a naked-eye object at maximum, even reaching mag 2 on rare occasions. At minimum it is below mag 10 and the variation has a period of about 332 days, taking three months to rise and seven months to decline. The star is a supergiant M6 type about 424×10^6 km across attended by a B-type binary companion in a 14-year orbit. The B star appears to interact with matter ejected from the pulsating supergiant.

Mira radiates 3·5 times as much energy at maximum brightness as it does at minimum and the star is the prototype for the class of long-period (or Mira) variables. Other interesting stars are β, Deneb Kaitos, a K1 type with mag 2.02, and α, Menkar, a M2 with mag 2·54.

Chamaeleon

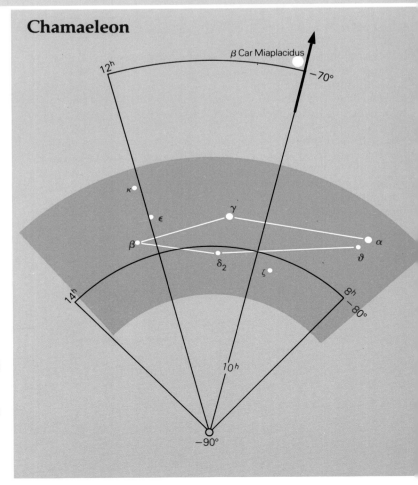

Chamaeleon Chamaeleontis Cha *Chameleon*

The constellation is probably best found by locating β and ω Carinae, which lie to the north. The constellation was one of a series named by Bayer very early in the 17th century. The brightest stars in the groups are of mag 4, and δ and ε Chamaeleontis are visual binaries.

---- Ecliptic
• double star
⊙ variable star > mag. 5
○ variable star < mag. 5
○ galaxy
◉ galactic nebula
◇ planetary nebula
⊕ globular cluster
○ open cluster

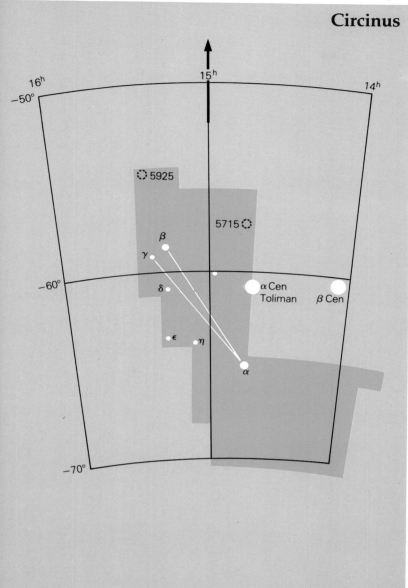

Circinus

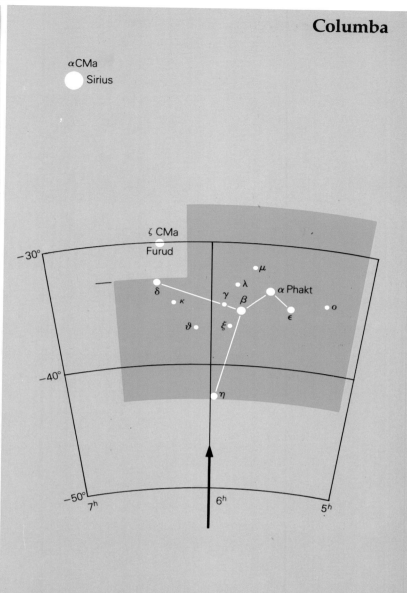

Columba

Circinus Circini Cir *Compass*

This constellation occupies a small region of the southern sky. It appears to form an elongated triangle and is flanked by Triangulum Australe, Norma, Lupus, Centaurus, Musca and Apus. Had it not been separated by Lacaille in 1763 (when he contributed 14 constellations to the charts) it would more properly be seen as a part of the constellation of Centaurus branching, perhaps, from α Centauri, the closest star system to the Sun. In any event, positive location of the two main stars in Centaurus helps with the identification of Circinus. The only really interesting star in this group is α Circini, a double (mags 3·4 and 8·8) of yellow and reddish appearance respectively.

Columba Columbae Col *Dove*

This southern constellation was originally named Columba Noae, which literally translated means the Dove of Noah. The abbreviated expression 'Columba' has now become the official title.

The only two stars of interest are α, Phakt and β Wezn. Phakt is a B8 star with an apparent mag of 2·64 and an absolute mag of −0·06 and is about 140 light years away. Wezn is of mag 3·2 and lies at the centre of the irregular 'T' formed by the constellation.

Coma Berenices

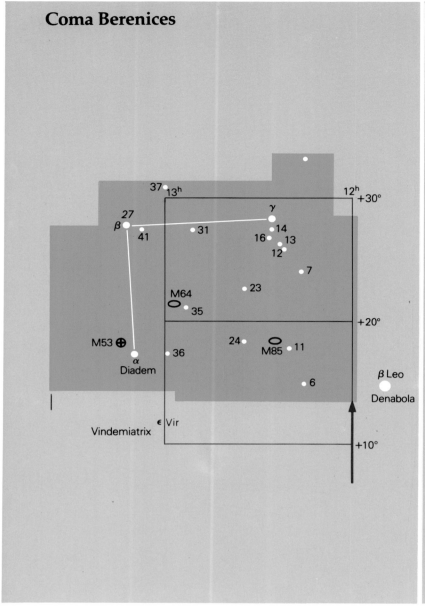

Corona Australis

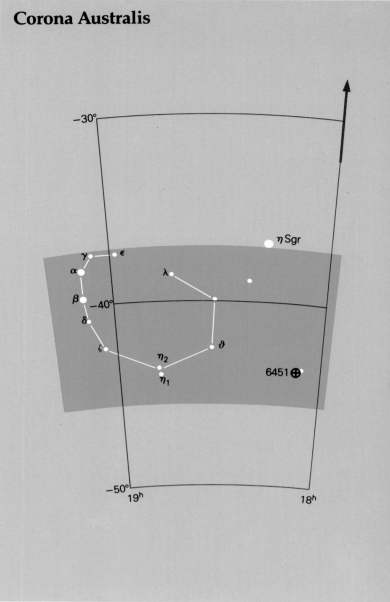

Coma Berenices Comae Berenices Com
Berenice's Hair

This constellation was added by Tycho Brahe in the 17th century and is flanked by Ursa Major, Leo, Virgo, Boötes and Canis Venatici, lying between RA 11 hr 55 min–13 hr 35 min and Dec 14–34. The origin of the name lies in Ptolemaic Egypt when a Pharaoh's sister, Berenice, promised to offer her severed hair to Venus if her husband returned safe from the Syrian wars. He did, but the locks were lost from the temple of Venus and the story was developed that Jupiter had removed them to form the constellation.

There are no stars greater than mag 4·5 in Coma Berenices but the north galactic pole lies close to a line connecting β and γ and the region is rich in extragalactic nebulae. Since it lies far above the galactic plane there are many external galaxies.

Corona Australis Coronae Australis CrA
Southern Crown

The constellation was one of Ptolemy's original group of 48 drawn up in the second century AD. It lies between the major constellations of Sagittarius and Scorpius. Corona Australis forms an arc apparently lying within the embrace of Sagittarius.

Corona Australis can be found by first locating the stars α, β and ε in Sagittarius. The constellation is then found lying within this triangle. It has been named because of its similarity to Corona Borealis which lies in the northern celestial hemisphere. No prominent objects lie within the constellation and the brightest stars are of mag 4.

Corona Borealis Coronae Borealis CrB
Northern Crown

This group looks very much like a more luminous, northerly duplicate of the Corona Australis, flanked by Boötes in the west.

The brightest star in the group is α, Gemma (or Alphecca) an eclipsing variable with a mean mag of 2·23 and a period of 17·4 days. The A0 type star is 76 light years away and has an absolute mag of 0·4. The star R Coronae Borealis is the prototype of a class of irregular variables. At random intervals it fades from its normal brightness (6·3), dropping by several magnitudes. This process is caused by absorption by carbon particles in the stellar atmosphere, and not due to an eclipsing companion. It may be observed with binoculars.

Corvus Corvi Crv *Crow*

Shaped rather like a kite this southern constellation seems to form the south-western corner of Virgo. The constellation is one of the original 48 groups.

The four brightest stars, γ, β, δ and ε, are all brighter than mag 3·1 although the fifth star in order of apparent mag is α. An alpha designation usually applies to the brightest star in a group. Star γ, Gienah, is a mag 2·59 B8 type at a distance of 450 light years and absolute mag of −3.1. β is a mag 2·66 G5 type (very similar to the Sun) at 108 light years. Star δ is a double (mags 2·7 and 8·26) with the secondary sometimes called 'The Raven'. ε is a mag 3·04 K3 object at 140 light years distance.

Ecliptic
double star
variable star > mag. 5

○ variable star < mag. 5
○ galaxy
◉ galactic nebula

◇ planetary nebula
⊕ globular cluster
○ open cluster

Corona Borealis

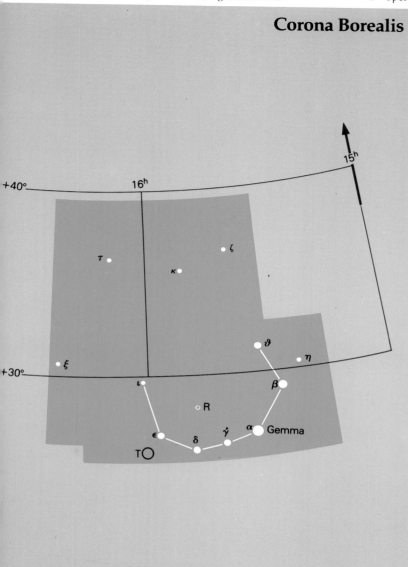

Crux

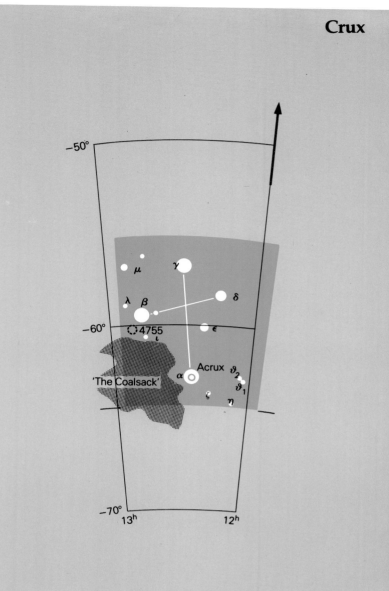

Corvus   Crater

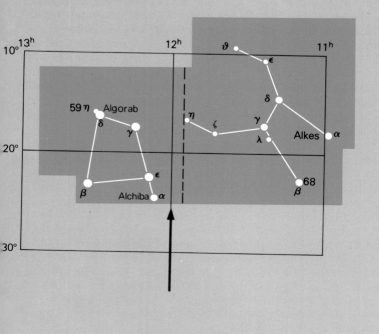

Crater Crateris Crt *Cup*

This is a southern sky constellation flanked by Leo, Virgo, Sextans, Hydra and Corvus, lying between RA 10 hr 50 min–11 hr 55 min and Dec −6 – −25. It is very inconspicuous but, nevertheless, one of Ptolemy's original 48 constellations. All the stars are of mag 4 or less.

Crux Crucis Cru *Cross*

Crux is the smallest constellation between RA 11 hr 55 min–12 hr 55 min and Dec −55 – −64. It is surrounded on three sides by Centaurus with Musca to the south. The Southern Cross was added to the list of constellations in the 17th century, and is most famous for its almost exact axial alignment with the south celestial pole.

The prime star is α, Acrux, actually a triple system with components of mag 1·6, 2·1 and 4·9. The brighter pair is seen as a single source at mag 0·87 at a distance of 370 light years with absolute mags of −3·9 and −3·4. Both are class B stars. β, Mimosa, is even further away, at 490 light years, and being a B0 star it has an absolute mag of −4·6. γ is mag 1·68 at a distance of 220 light years and is a M3 star of absolute mag −2·5. δ, Crucis, is a variable star with a mean mag of 2·81 (2·78–2·84) at a distance of 570 light years.

Star ε is of mag 3 and seems ill-placed in this symmetrical system. In the area between α and β and close to red κ Cru, lies the Coalsack, a famous dark nebula filled with inert dust and gas.

Constellation maps

Cygnus

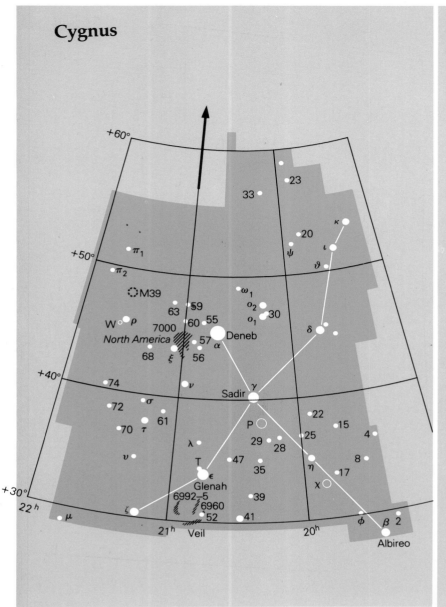

Delphinus

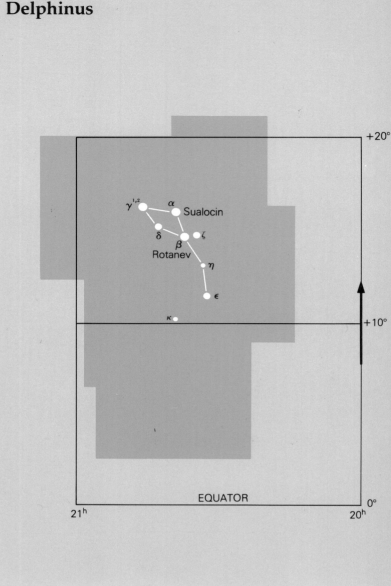

Cygnus Cygni Cyg *Swan*

For an obvious reason Cygnus is sometimes referred to as the 'Northern Cross'. α, Deneb, is one of the brightest stars in the sky and with a mag of 1·26 and a distance of 1600 light years, the star is seen to be an A2 type with an absolute mag of −7·1, 30 000 times the luminosity of the Sun.

One of the most rewarding sights in the sky is the optical double β, Albireo, of mag 3·07, a rich blue K type star 410 light years away accompanied by a golden partner of mag 5. Most of the stars in this constellation are intrinsicaly bright. An interesting star can be found about halfway between γ Cyg, Sadr, and Albireo. It is χ Cyg, a long-period variable (period 409 days) similar to Mira, *o* Ceti. It varies between mag 4 and 14. Like most variables of this type, although basically regular, it shows considerable fluctuations in the form of the light-curve.

Delphinus Delphini Del *Dolphin*

Delphinus lies in a part of the sky that includes several constellations with 'watery' connections (Aquarius, Capricornus, and so on). It does bear some resemblance to a dolphin, although it has been likened to a diamond-shaped kite. The two brightest stars are α, Sualocin and β, Rotanev. These names derive from the reversal of the name Nicolaus Venator, the Latinized version of Nicolo Cacciatore, assistant to Piazzi at Palermo Observatory. The star γ is a well-known telescopic double.

Dorado Doradus Dor *Dorado*

This constellation is one of the star groups named by Bayer in 1603. It represents the fish often incorrectly called a 'dolphin', and it is often (also incorrectly) said to be a swordfish. There are no particularly outstanding stars and the only one of note in the group is α Doradus of mag 3·5. However, the constellation does contain the Large Magellanic Cloud (LMC) in its southern sector. This appears as a faint patch more than 1 hr of longitude in width and centred on Dec −70.

The Large Magellanic Cloud is so-called because it was first noted by Europeans during the course of Magellan's expedition early in the 16th century. Visible to the keen, naked eye, the LMC is an irregular galaxy, the nearest system to the Milky Way galaxy, at a distance of about $1·7 \times 10^5$ light-years. An extremely bright star, S Doradus varies between mag 8·2 and 9·4. At the distance of the LMC it has an absolute mag greater than −8.

Ecliptic
double star
variable star > mag. 5

○ variable star < mag. 5
◯ galaxy
◉ galactic nebula

◇ planetary nebula
⊕ globular cluster
○ open cluster

Dorado

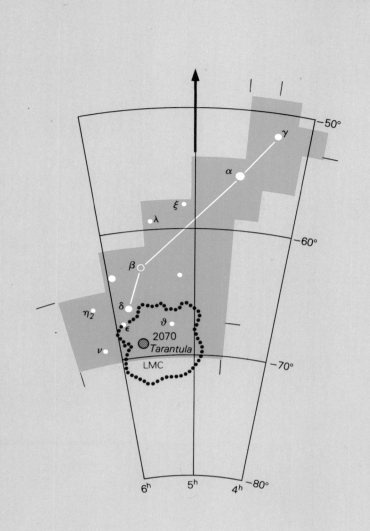

Draco

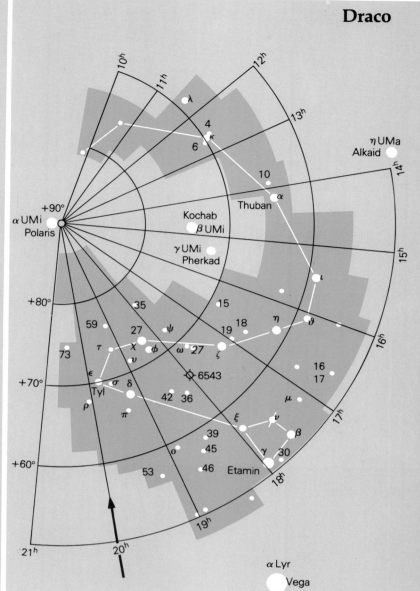

Draco Draconis Dra *Dragon*

Draco is one of the oldest recorded constellations and was known to the Egyptians, Greeks, Chinese and Arabs under various names. It spreads in a long chain of fairly isolated stars around a large portion of the northern circumpolar sky.

The brightest star in Draco is γ, Etamin, a mag 2·21 K5 object more than 100 light years away. In 3000 BC α, Thuban, a spectroscopic binary of mag 3·6, was the pole star but subsequent precession of the equinoxes has now moved Polaris to this position. β, of mag 2·77, is actually a double star with component mags of 2·7 and 11·5. Draco contains the north pole of the ecliptic lying roughly between stars δ and ζ on the 18 hr RA arc.

Equuleus

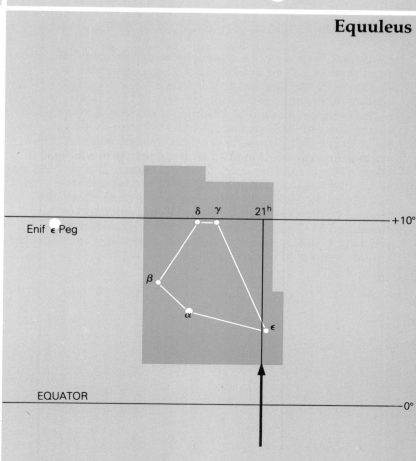

Equuleus Equulei Equ *Little Horse*

Equuleus is a small constellation between Pegasus and Delphinus. Although it is a very inconspicuous group, the constellation is a member of the old list known to the Babylonians. It is best found looking to the west of ε Pegasi, Enif. All the stars in Equuleus are faint, α being just about mag 4, and β is about 1 mag fainter. Nothing of great interest is seen in the constellation but it is well located between Pegasus, Delphinus and Aquarius.

Eridanus

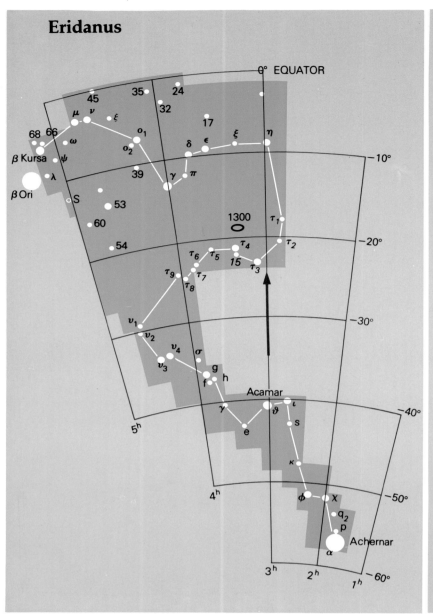

Fornax

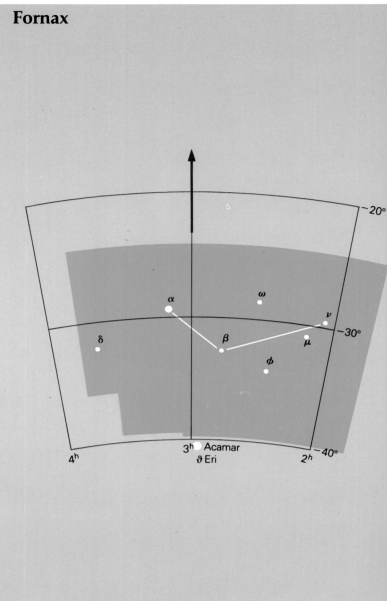

Eridanus Eridani Eri *River Eridanus*

Eridanus is supposedly a representation of the celestial equivalent of a river; the Nile to the Egyptians, and the Euphrates to the Babylonians. It snakes an exceedingly sinuous path south of the equator.

The brightest star in the group, α, Achernar, is not visible to observers in the northern latitudes because of the extreme range in celestial latitude covered by the constellation. The star has a mag of 0·53 and it lies at a distance of 120 light years with an absolute mag of −2·3. β, Kursa, is a mag 2·8 star of A3 class with an absolute mag of 0·9 and it lies at a distance of 80 light years. Star θ Eridani Acamar, was once the end of the constellation, before it was extended on to Achernar. It is a triple system with the brightest member visible as a yellow dwarf to the naked eye and two extremely faint companions, one of which is a red dwarf and the other a white dwarf.

Fornax Fornacis For *Furnace*

This constellation once formed part of the straggling constellation of Eridanus. The name Fornax (Latin for furnace) was given to the constellation by the astronomer Lacaille in the mid-18th century. After naming a nearby group 'The Sculptor', he proceeded to assign this craftsman various tools, including a furnace, with which to accomplish his assumed tasks.

The three stars making up the main configuration take on the appearance of a flattened 'V' and lie in the centre of the rectangular area covered by this constellation. No stars brighter than mag 4 are found in this region.

Ecliptic ----   ○ variable star < mag. 5   ◇ planetary nebula
double star ◆   ○ galaxy   ⊕ globular cluster
variable star > mag. 5 ⊙   ◍ galactic nebula   ◌ open cluster

Gemini

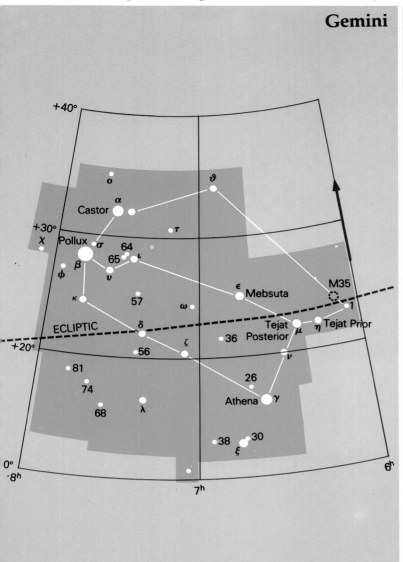

Grus

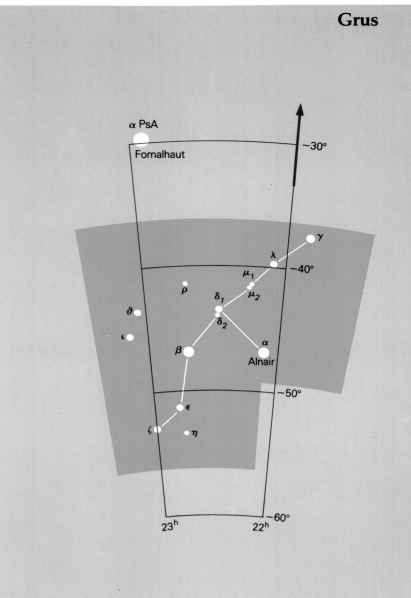

Gemini Geminorum Gem *Twins*

Gemini is one of the constellations of the zodiac, where it lies between Taurus and Cancer.

Gemini is most famous for the stars α, Castor, and β, Pollux. Castor, the fainter, appears as a star of mag 1·62. It actually consists of three spectroscopic binaries (mag 1·97, 2·95 and 9·08). All six stars from a single, complex system, which is at a distance of about 45 light years. Pollux is the brightest member of the constellation, a mag 1·16 K0 star 35 light years distant but intrinsically dimmer than the Castor system.

Alhena is an A star of mag 1·93 at a distance of 105 light years. μ, Tejat Posterior, is a variable with a mean mag of 2·92 at 160 light years and ε, Mebsuta, is a mag 3 G8 star more than 1000 light years from the Sun. The constellation includes the beautiful open star cluster, M35, best seen with low-power binoculars. Neptune and Pluto were discovered when passing through Gemini.

Grus Gruis Gru *Crane*

Grus is a 17th-century constellation probably added by Bayer, although it was known as 'The Flamingo' by some authors.

The most prominent stars are α, Alnair, a mag 1·76 B5 star 65 light years distant, and β, a slightly variable mean mag 2·17 M3 star nearly 300 light years away. Star γ Al Dhanab is a B8 object of mag 3·03 and is in fact the brightest of all three, intrinsically mag −3·1 but reduced in apparent mag by its 550 light year distance. A 4th mag star, δ, is a naked eye double with two components designated δ^1 and δ^2.

Hercules

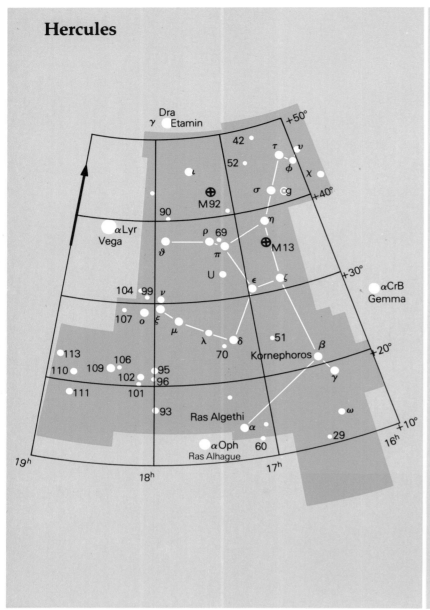

Horologium

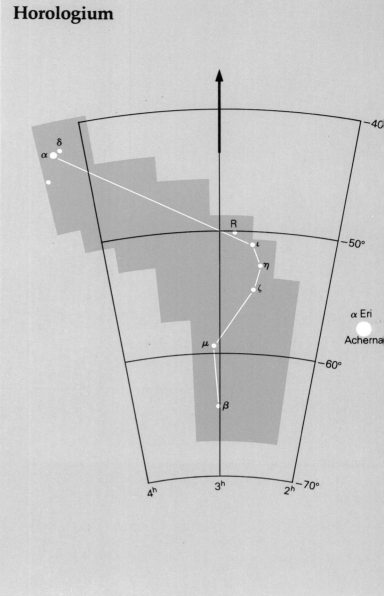

Hercules Herculis Her *Hercules*

This is one of the early constellations, named after the mythical hero. The central position, 'The Keystone', ε, ζ, π and η is easily found between Corona Borealis and Lyra.

The most important star, α, Ras Algethi, is a cool red M type supergiant variable of mean mag 3·5 with a mag 6·1 G type companion. Ras Algethi has been estimated to be up to $4·5 \times 10^{10}$ km in radius which, if true, makes it the largest known star. β, Kornephoros, is a G type 2·8 mag star 100 light years distant, while ζ and μ Herculis are multiple systems.

An interesting globular cluster, M13, can be found between η and ζ. It is believed to contain more than 10^5 stars in a group 100 light years across. The cluster is about 34 000 light years away, but is just visible to the naked eye.

Horologium Horologii Hor *Clock*

Horologium was added to the list of constellations by Lacaille in the mid-18th century. It runs roughly parallel to the end of Eridanus, and can be located from Achernar. In fact its brightest components lie between Eridanus and Caelum.

The most prominent star in Horologium is of mag 3·8 and there is nothing of significance in the rest of the sky occupied by this constellation. It is said to represent an old-fashioned pendulum clock, as used in early observatories.

----	Ecliptic	○	variable star < mag. 5	◇	planetary nebula
⬤	double star	○	galaxy	⊕	globular cluster
⊙	variable star > mag. 5	◉	galactic nebula	○	open cluster

Hydra

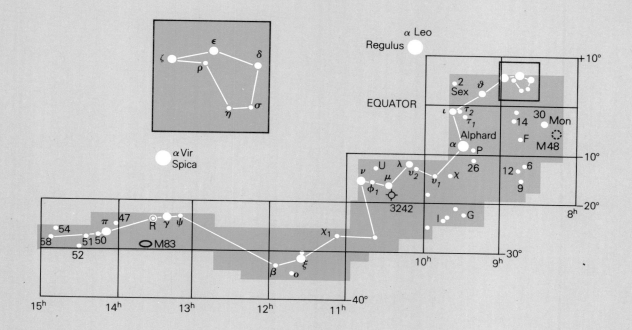

Hydra Hydrae Hya *Hydra (water monster)*

Hydra, the largest of the constellations, snakes a long path between RA 8 hr 10 min and RA 15 hr. The 'head' of the monster is a small asterism of just six stars with only two greater than mag 4.

α, Alphard, is a red K4 type mag 1·98 object with an absolute mag of −0·3 located 94 light years from the Sun and found south-east of the head. ε is one of the two prominent stars in the head and is actually four stars of mags 3·7, 5·2, 6·8 and 12·1. On the borders of Hydra and Centaurus, just below star γ is the M83 galaxy catalogued as NGC 5253 while M68, a globular cluster, can be found between stars γ and ζ. The bright cluster M48 was 'lost' for many years as Messier had made an error in his original, published catalogue.

Hydrus

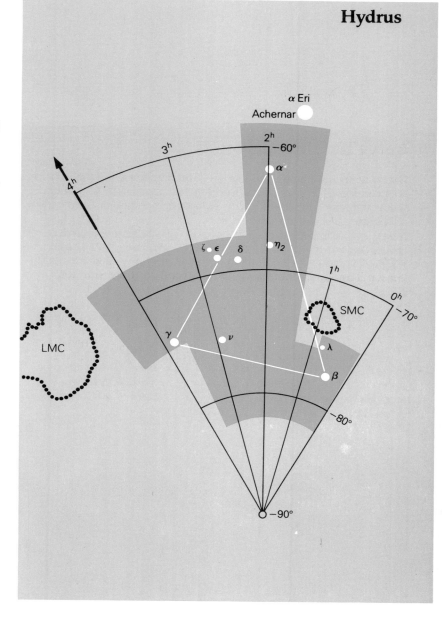

Hydrus Hydri Hyi *Sea serpent*

This constellation was introduced in the Bayer catalogue of 1603. It is a fairly inconspicuous constellation, largely consisting of a triangle of bright stars, south of Achernar. It also includes part of the Small Magellanic Cloud (SMC) but most of this lies in neighbouring Tucana.

β Hydri is a mag 2·78 star of G1 type at a distance of just over 20 light years. Star α, although not the brightest, is a mag 2·84 F0 type more than 30 light years distant.

Constellation maps

Indus

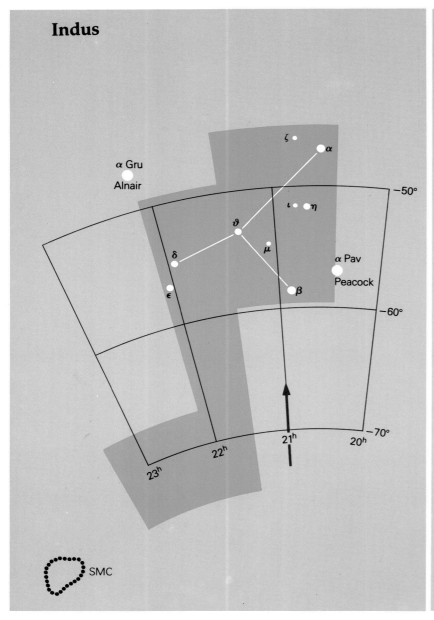

Lacerta

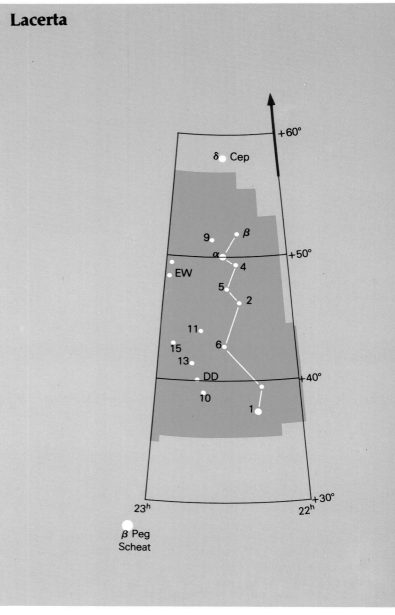

Indus Indi Ind *Indian*

Indus is an inconspicuous constellation in the southern sky. It was named by Bayer in his famous atlas, published in 1603. It is fairly easily identified, lying between the stars α Gruis and α Pavonis.

The star α Indi is a mag 3·2 object, the brightest in the constellation. β Indi is close to mag 4, and the other three major stars are all below 4th mag. ε Indi is one of the nearest stars to the Sun, about 11·4 light years distant with a mag of 4·7 and absolute mag of 7·0.

Lacerta Lacertae Lac *Lizard*

Named by Hevelius in 1690, Lacerta lies to the south of δ Cephei, the famous variable star. This constellation contains only eight bright members, all of mag 4, with several variable stars. No other interesting objects are contained within the boundaries of this northern constellation.

Leo Leonis Leo *Lion*

Leo is one of the oldest constellations, and was recognized by many ancient civilizations, including those in Babylonia, Egypt and Greece. It was then close to the position of the Sun at summer solstice.

The most interesting objects in the constellation are α, Regulus, which is a double (mags 1·36 and 10·8) of B7 spectrum, absolute mag −0·7, and lying at a distance of 84 light years. γ, Algieba, is a spectacular double, appearing yellow and green. The combined magnitude is 1·99 and the pair lie at a distance of nearly 200 light years. β, Denebola, is a mag 2·14 A3 type just 43 light years away.

One of the brightest, intrinsically, in the constellation is ε, Asad Australis, a mag 2·99 G0 type star with an absolute mag of −2·1 which is 340 light years away. As would be expected from its close proximity to Coma Berenices and Virgo, Leo contains many external galaxies visible above the galactic plane.

Leo Minor Leonis Minoris LMi *Little Lion*

This constellation was added to the list by Hevelius late in the 17th century and lies between Ursa Major and Leo.

The main star, carrying the unusual designation β, is a mag 4 object as are the remaining three moderately bright stars of this constellation. Leo Minor is very inconspicuous and contains little of interest to the amateur apart from a few variable stars. A number of faint, distant galaxies are visible in large telescopes.

Ecliptic
double star
variable star > mag. 5

○ variable star < mag. 5
○ galaxy
○ galactic nebula

◇ planetary nebula
⊕ globular cluster
○ open cluster

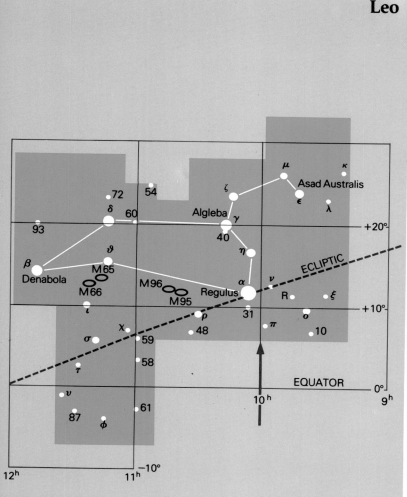

Leo

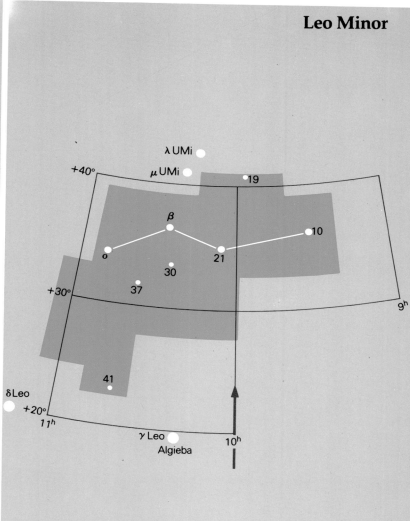

Leo Minor

Lepus Leporis Lep *Hare*

Lepus is one of the 48 constellations recognized by Ptolemy. It supposedly represented one of the creatures hunted by Orion, lying, as it does, south of that constellation.

The main star, α, Arneb, is a mag 2·58 F0 type with an absolute mag of −4·6 and a distance of 900 light years. Intrinsically less bright, β, Nihal, is a mag 2·81 G5 star (absolute mag 0·1) lying just 113 light years distant. The star is a double with a mag 9·4 companion.

The star ε Leporis is a mag 3·2 object while μ Leporis is of mag 3·3. A 430-day-period variable, R Leporis, is located in the direction of Eridanus and being of mag 6 at its brightest it is just visible to the naked eye but is totally invisible when it dims to mag 10·4.

The M79 globular cluster is found south-west of Nihal; the distance from that star is equal to the distance separating α and β and on a line extended beyond these two stars.

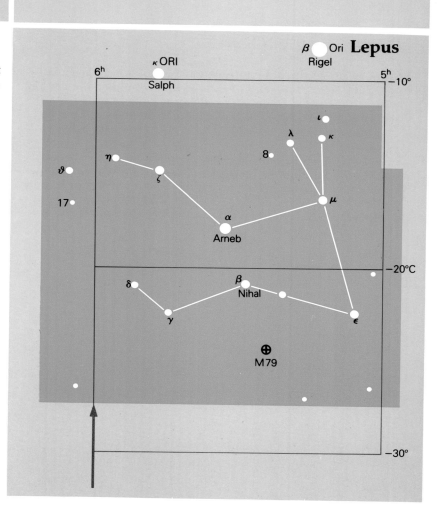

Constellation maps

Key to constellations
scale of magnitude
0 1 2 3 4 5

Libra

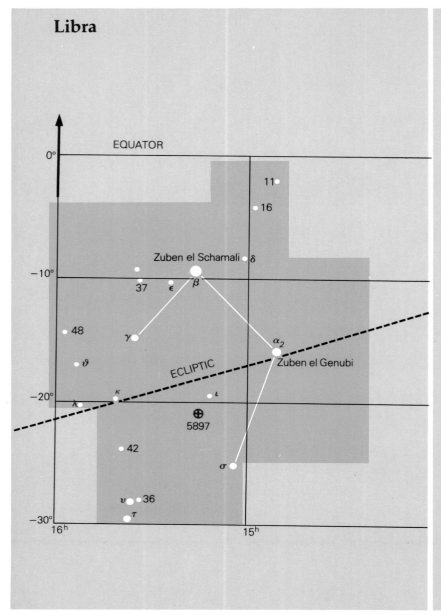

Lupus

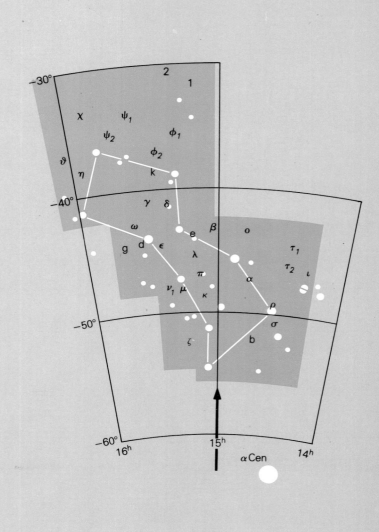

Libra Librae Lib *Scales*

Libra is one of the old constellations, and once formed part of Scorpius, the constellation to the east. It straddles the ecliptic and is therefore a zodiacal constellation. The brightest star in the group is the mag 2·61 β, Zuben el Schamali, of B8 type, absolute mag −0·6 located 140 light years from the solar system.

Star α, Zuben el Genubi, actually a double, is an A3 class object with an absolute mag of 1·2. Its companion is said by some to be a vivid green even to the naked eye and it has an apparent mag of 5·2. Several noted astronomers, amateur and professional, have refuted this and the coloration seems to depend upon personal eyesight.

Lupus Lupi Lup *Wolf*

Lupus is an original constellation covering most of the region between the bright stars α Centauri, Toliman and α Scorpii, Antares.

The three brightest stars, α, β and γ are all brighter than mag 2·8 and all three exhibit B1 or B2 class spectra. Star α is a mag 2·3 object lying at a distance of 430 light years, and star β is of mag 2·69 at a distance of 540 light years. These have absolute mags of −3·3 and −3·4 respectively, intrinsically very bright sources. Star γ has a visual mag of 2·8, an absolute mag of −2·7, and is found to lie 570 light years from the Sun. This latter star is a double with individual mags of 3·5 and 3·7.

Star ζ Lupi is another double with mag 3·4 and 3·8 components, and star η is a third double with components exhibiting mags 3·5 and 7·7.

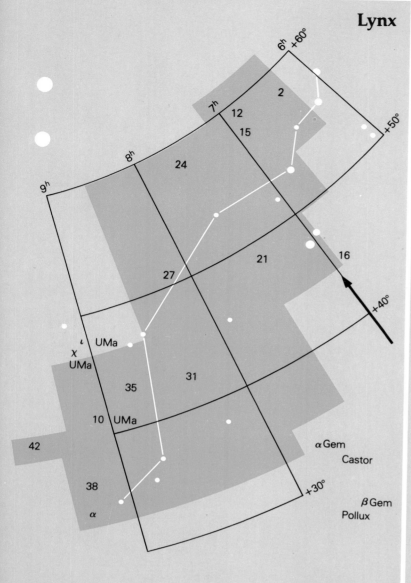

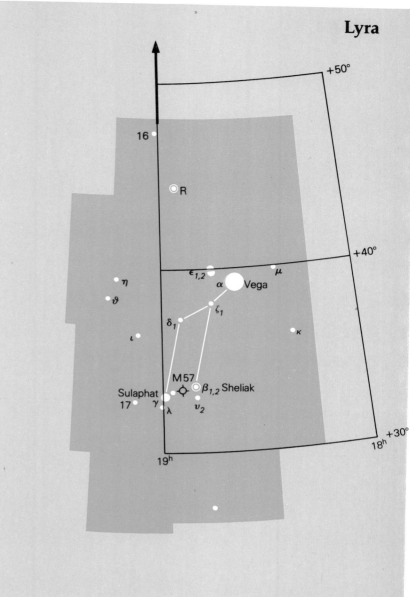

Lynx Lyncis Lyn *Lynx*

Towards the end of the 17th century, Hevelius reputedly named this constellation, Lynx, because of the remarkable eyesight demanded of any observer studying this apparently barren area. It lies between 3 important constellations (Auriga, Gemini, Ursa Major) and 3 insignificant ones (Camelopardalis, Cancer, Leo Minor).

Star α Lyncis is a mag 3·2 object 180 light years away. The rest are less than mag 4 in brightness.

Lyra Lyrae Lyr *Lyre*

Lyra was one of the first constellations to be described. Star α, Vega, second brightest in the northern celestial hemisphere, is a class A0 object of mag 0·04 at a distance of 26 light years (absolute mag 0·5) with a mag 10 companion.

Star β, Sheliak, is an eclipsing variable (mags 3·4–4·1) with a mag 7·8 companion. These stars, each between 16×10^6 -24×10^6 km in radius, orbit each other with a separation of less than 5×10^6 km. Star ε is actually two stars, one of mag 4·6 with a mag 6·3 companion and one of mag 4·9 with a mag 5·2 companion. Each pair is a binary and the entire group is bound gravitationally. It is not unusual to find a multiple system of this nature and complex gravitational interactions can theoretically involve many stars.

Yet another double, ζ Lyrae, is found midway between δ and α with components of mag 4·2 and 5·5. Lyra incorporates a reported nova from 1919 due south of the midpoint between stars β and γ and a globular cluster, M56, south-west of star γ and in almost a direct line drawn from star α through γ.

The famous Ring Nebula, catalogued as M57 (NGC 6720) is located almost half way along a line drawn from γ to β. This is a classic planetary nebula and was caused by the central star of mag 15 shedding a shell of material.

Mensa

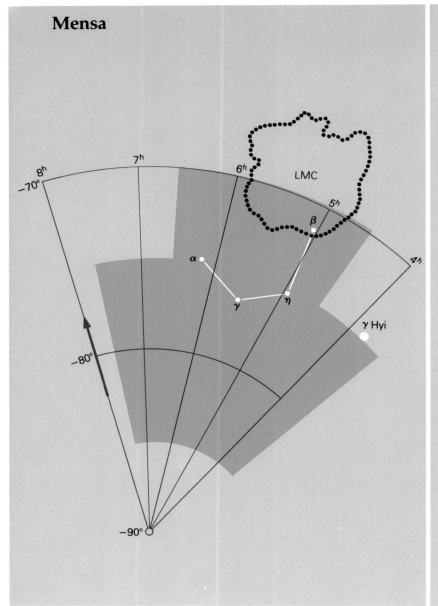

Microscopium

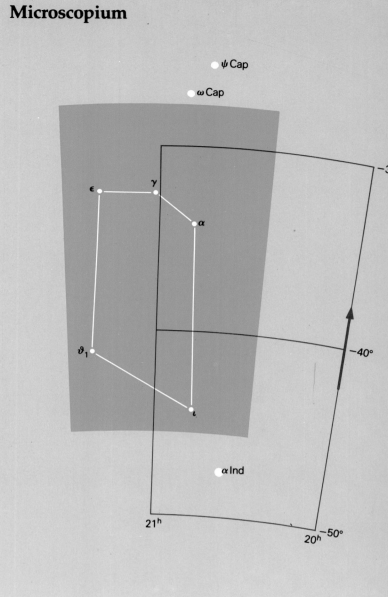

Mensa Mensae Men *Table (Mountain)*

This constellation was originally named Mons Mensa by Lacaille, whose observatory was at Cape Town in South Africa.

The constellation contains about 20 mag 5 stars but none of these is particularly interesting. The most notable claim to fame for this constellation comes from its partial occupation by a section of the LMC, itself more properly sited in Dorado. The faint star β is located in the centre of the Tarantula nebula, the most conspicuous feature of the Large Magellanic Cloud.

Microscopium Microscopii Mic *Microscope*

Microscopium is one of the few constellations that are rectangular and have straight boundaries. Once again, it is an insignificant area named by Lacaille. There is little of observational interest in the entire constellation.

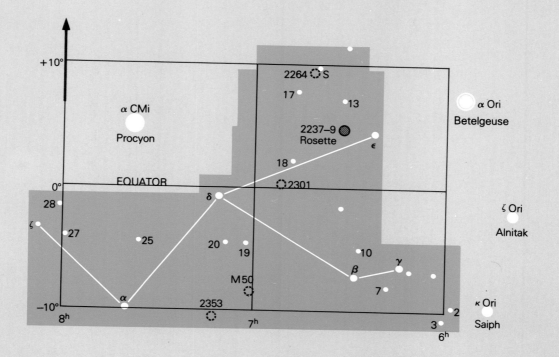

Ecliptic
double star
variable star > mag. 5

variable star < mag. 5
galaxy
galactic nebula

planetary nebula
globular cluster
open cluster

Monoceros Monocerotis Mon *Unicorn*

This constellation was named by Hevelius in his atlas published in 1690. It lies across the celestial equator, and is also crossed by the main band of the Milky Way.

None of the main stars in the constellation are very bright, α, γ and δ all being approximately magnitude 4·1. M50 is an open cluster, best observed with a small telescope. NGC 2264 is visible to the naked eye and lies close to the irregular variable S Mon. The famous and beautiful Rosette Nebula is NGC 2237–9.

Musca Muscae Mus *Fly*

This constellation is sometimes known as Musca Australis (Southern Fly) and is one of those entered in the 1603 Bayer catalogue. It lies to the south of α Crucis and the famous 'Coalsack' dark nebula.

The star α Muscae is a mag 2·7 variable (mag 2·66–2·73) of B3 spectral type (absolute mag −2·9) situated 430 light years from the solar system. Star β Muscae, mag 3·06, is a B3 double with component mags of 3·7 and 4·1 and the system lies at a distance of about 470 light years.

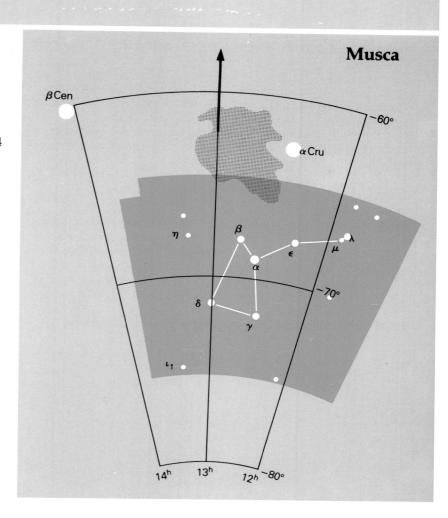

Constellation maps

Norma

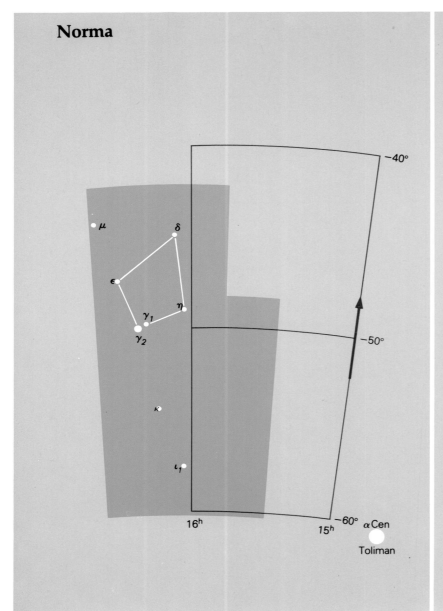

Octans

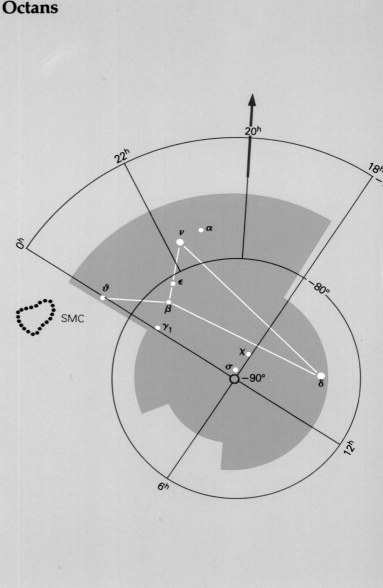

Norma Normae Nor *Level (square)*

This southern constellation was originally called Norma et Regula (the 'square and level') and was intended by Lacaille to represent some of the tools used by Sculptor.

There are no particularly interesting stars in the constellation and all are dimmer than mag 4. An interesting open cluster – NGC 6067 – is located on a line projected from ε through γ and lies close to the star $\varkappa$

Octans Octantis Oct *Octant*

Octans is the constellation that contains the southern celestial pole. It was named by Lacaille, being originally 'Hadley's Octant' from the important navigational instrument, later replaced by the sextant (also represented in the sky).

The brightest star, ν, is mag 3·7 and the closest star to the actual pole is σ, a dim object of nearly mag 6·0. Apart from the important relationship with the celestial sphere, the constellation contains little of observational interest.

Ophiuchus Ophiuchi Oph
Ophiuchus (serpent bearer)

When the zodiac was originally named, the ecliptic did not cross Ophiuchus, so the constellation was not included. Due to precession, the Sun now spends quite a long period in the constellation, which also lies across the celestial equator.

The most prominent star in the constellation is Ras Alhague, north of the celestial equator and just south of Hercules. The star is a mag 2·09 A5 type located 58 light years from the solar system with an absolute mag of 0·8. Star η, Sabik, is a mag 2·46 object, actually a double with components of mag 3·0 and 3·4, with an A3 spectrum and an absolute mag of 1·4 at a distance of 70 light years.

Star ζ, Han, found almost due north-east from Sabik, is a mag 2·57 09 type star with an absolute mag of −4·3. It lies at a distance of more than 500 light years. At the other end of the spectral scale the observer can find δ, Yed Prior, on the boundary with the constellation Serpens Caput. This is an M1 type object with mag 2·72, absolute mag −0·5, and a separation distance of 140 light years.

Star β, Cheleb, another interesting object, is a K2 type mag 2·77 object with absolute mag of −0·1 at a distance of 124 light years. Three faint globular clusters can be seen located within the area of a triangle set up by straight lines joining Yed Prior and stars γ and μ. These clusters, M10, M12 and M14, are all at extremely remote distances. Globular cluster M9 is adjacent to a line joining stars η and ζ. M19 is south-west of θ.

Ecliptic
double star
variable star > mag. 5
variable star < mag. 5
galaxy
galactic nebula
planetary nebula
globular cluster
open cluster

Ophiuchus

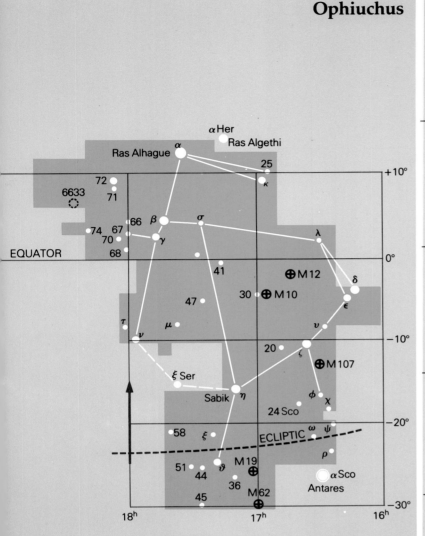

Orion

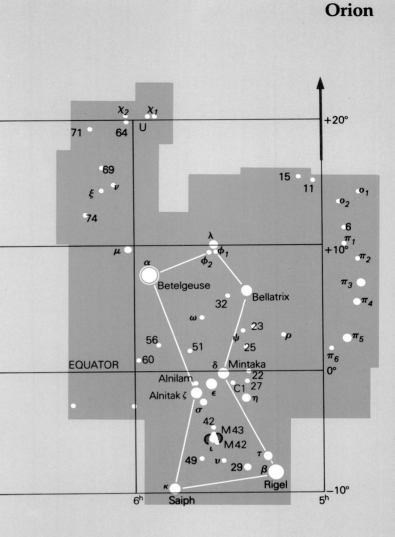

Orion Orionis Ori *Orion*

This prominent and interesting constellation lies across the celestial equator, so it is well-known to all astronomers. The three most interesting stars in this group form the famous belt of Orion: ζ, Alnitak, ε, Alnilam, and δ, Mintaka. Alnitak is a remote double with component mags of 1·9 and 4·05 (system mag of 1·79) and absolute mag of −6·6; Alnilam is a super-giant star of type B0 at a distance of 1600 light years (as is Alnitak) with an absolute mag of −6·8; and Mintaka is an eclipsing variable (mag 2·2–2·35) with a mag 6·47 companion and a period slightly less than six days.

The upper part of the constellation is marked by α, Betelgeuse, (mag 0·5–1·1 variable, class M2) and γ, Bellatrix, (mag 1·64, B2 type). To the south lie κ, Saiph (mag 2·06, B0 type), and β, Rigel (mag 0·08, B8 type of absolute mag −7·1, distance 900 light years). A striking quadruple system is that of σ Orionis, southwest of Alnitak. Slightly farther south lies the Great Orion Nebula, faintly visible to the naked eye, and a magnificent sight in any telescope. The vast cloud of gas is largely illuminated by the stars of the Trapezium, θ Orionis, all young stars between 6th and 8th magnitude.

Pavo Pavonis Pav *Peacock*

This constellation is one of those named by Bayer in 1603. The brightest star is α Pavonis, on the very border of Indus and Telescopium. It is a mag 1·95 B3 star (absolute mag −2·9) and is 310 light years away. κ is a mag 4·0–5·5 Cepheid variable with a period of just over nine days. There is one interesting globular cluster, NGC 6752.

Pavo

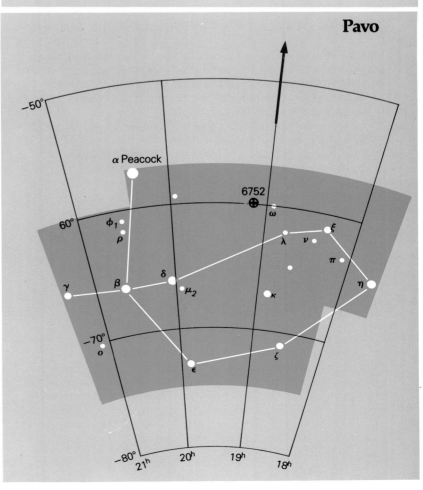

| 0 | 1 | 2 | 3 | 4 | 5 |

Pegasus

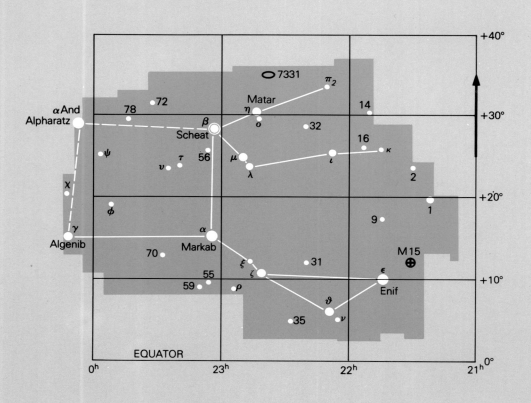

Pegasus Pegasi Peg *Pegasus (winged horse)*

Pegasus is another very interesting constellation and it can be recognized by the prominent square formed by three member stars (β, α and γ) and α, Alpheratz, in the neighbouring constellation of Andromeda. Alpheratz lies on the very border of the two designated areas.

The three corners of the square of Pegasus that lie in this constellation are all above mag 3 and are good observational objects. Star β, Scheat, is a large M2 variable red giant (absolute mag – 1·5) at a distance of 210 light years and may range between 2·4 and 2·7. Star α, Markab, is a white B9 of mag 2·5 and γ is a mag 2·84 B2 type (absolute mag −3·4) at distances of 110 and 570 light years respectively. North-west of β lies η, Matar, a mag 2·95 G8 star.

Star ε, Enif, in Pegasus is a mag 2·3 K2 type star with a mag 9 companion. Enif is nearly 800 light years away and has an absolute mag of −4·6. North-west of ε lies M15 a 6th magnitude globular cluster.

Perseus Persei Per *Perseus*

Perseus, one of the earliest named constellations, lies between Cassiopeia and Auriga in the northern Milky Way.

The most interesting object in Perseus is β, Algol, an eclipsing binary and a prototype of this class of variable star. Algol, a mag 2·06–3·28 B8 type star, lies at a distance of 105 light years and is accompanied by a companion of similar size just 1.6×10^7 km away. The period of the components is just under three days but a third, much smaller, star orbits the binary system in 23 months.

The brightest star in Perseus is α, Mirfak, a giant F5 of mag 1·8 (absolute mag −4·4) surrounded by several much fainter stars. ζ Persei is a double with mag 3 and 9 components; ε is another double with mags 3 and 8 and ρ Persei is a mag 3·2–3·8 variable. The open clusters h and χ are magnificent objects in low-power instruments. M34 is a very loose open cluster, while M76, near ϕ is a faint planetary nebula.

Phoenix Phoenicis Phe *Phoenix*

This is another Bayer constellation and it is named after the mythological bird that rose from the ashes following repeated burning. Phoenix is not very conspicuous and contains only three stars above mag 4. The brightest star in this assemblage is α, Ankaa, a mag 2·39 K0 type lying at a distance of 93 light years and an absolute mag of 0·1. Star β Phoenicis is a double with prime and secondary object mags of 4·1 each.

Star γ is a mag 4 object as is star ζ with a mag 8·4 companion. The constellation is best found by locating Achernar, a mag 0·53 star in Eridanus.

Pictor Pictoris Pic *Easel*

The constellation is found by locating the mag −0·73 star Canopus in the constellation Carina.

The only bright stars of note are α and β. Star α Pictoris is a mag 3·27 object and star β Pictoris is of mag 3·9. A nova which flared up in 1925. RR Pictoris, can be found adjacent to star α. It is still visible but a large telescope is required to see anything significant.

Ecliptic
○ variable star < mag. 5 ◇ planetary nebula
● double star
○ galaxy ⊕ globular cluster
⊙ variable star > mag. 5 ▨ galactic nebula ○ open cluster

Perseus

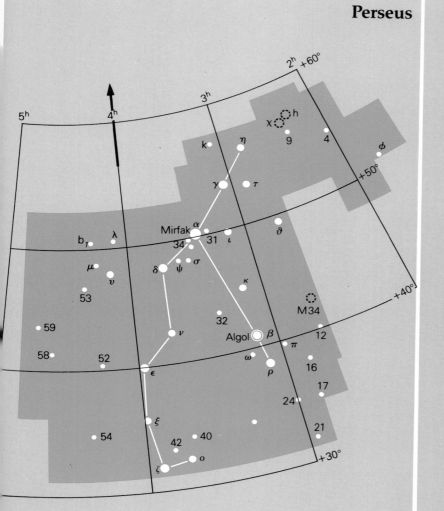

Pictor

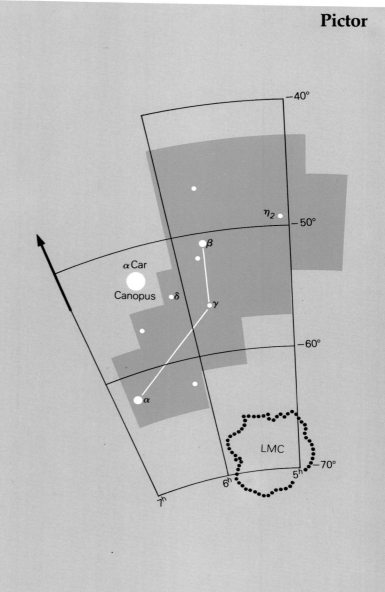

Phoenix

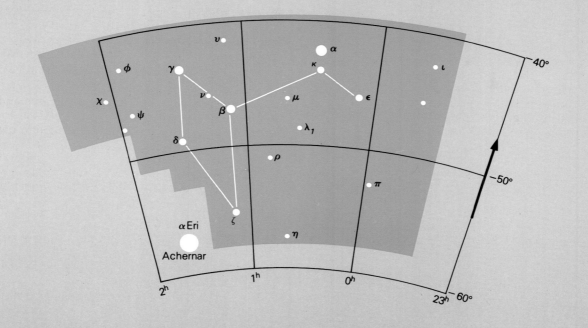

Pisces

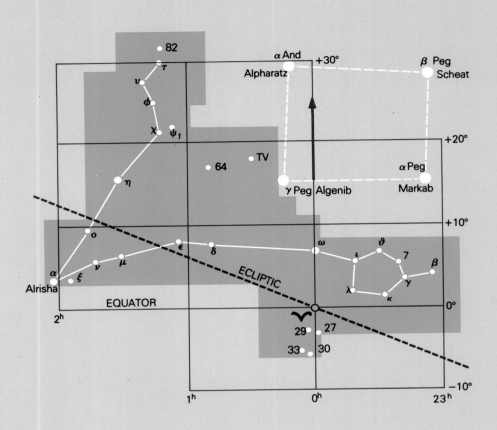

Pisces Piscium Psc *Fishes*

Although it is unspectacular, Pisces has been recognized as a zodiacal constellation since the days of the earliest civilizations. It lies on the southern and eastern sides of the great square of Pegasus. Due to precession, the vernal equinox, once in Aries, is now well into Pisces.

The most prominent object in Pisces is η Piscium (mag 3·9) followed by α, Alrisha, of mag 3·94, actually a double with mag 4·3 and 5·2 components. A galaxy recorded by Charles Messier, M74 in the catalogue, is found adjacent to star η.

---- Ecliptic
◦ variable star < mag. 5
◇ planetary nebula
• double star
○ galaxy
⊕ globular cluster
⊙ variable star > mag. 5
◍ galactic nebula
⬭ open cluster

Piscis Austrinus

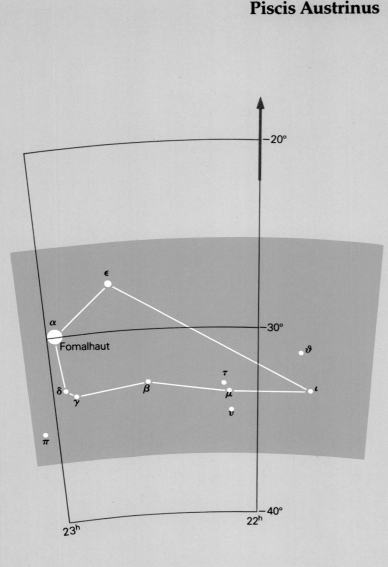

Puppis

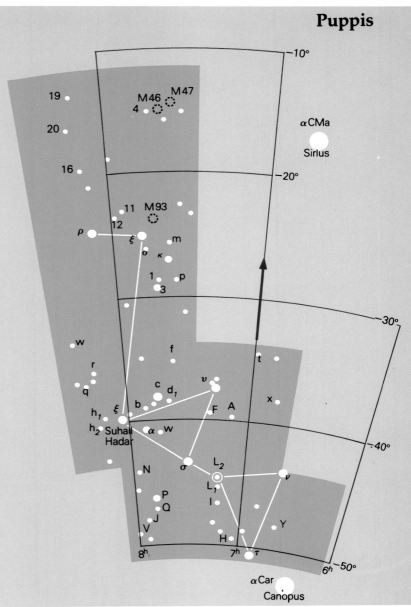

Piscis Austrinus Piscis Austrini PsA
Southern Fish

Piscis Austrinus, one of the originally named constellations, lies between Aquarius and Grus. The only really interesting object in the entire constellation is the magnificent white star Fomalhaut, an A3 type of mag 1·19 and absolute mag 2·0, lying at the comparatively close distance of 23 light years and 11 times as luminous as the Sun. All the remaining members of this constellation are below mag 3.

Puppis Puppis Pup *Stern (of a ship)*

Puppis was one of the three constellations that originally formed the sprawling and unwieldy Argo Navis – one of the 48 Ptolemaic constellations and now separated into Puppis, Carina and Vela. Puppis can be found best, like Pictor, by first locating Canopus (in the constellation of Carina) and seeking the pattern of stars which lies north of this.

The brightest star in the group is ζ, Suhail Hadar, with a mag of 2·23 at the tremendous distance (comparatively) of 2400 light years giving it an absolute mag of −7·1. It is a very hot, and rare type of star with an 05 spectrum. Stars L₁ and L₂ are an optical double. L₂ is variable, ranging between 3·4 and 6·2.

The only other moderately interesting star is τ, a mag 2·97 K0 type with absolute mag 0·1 at·a distance of 125 light years. There are several open clusters in the constellation, the brightest M47, being visible to the naked eye. M46 and M93 are fainter, but still striking objects to observe.

Key to constellations
scale of magnitude
0 1 2 3 4 5

Pyxis

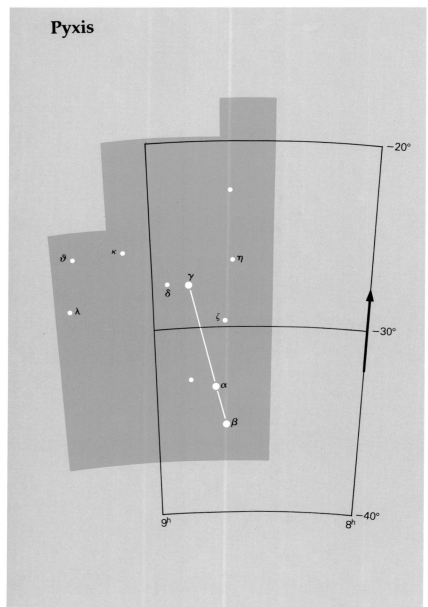

Sagitta

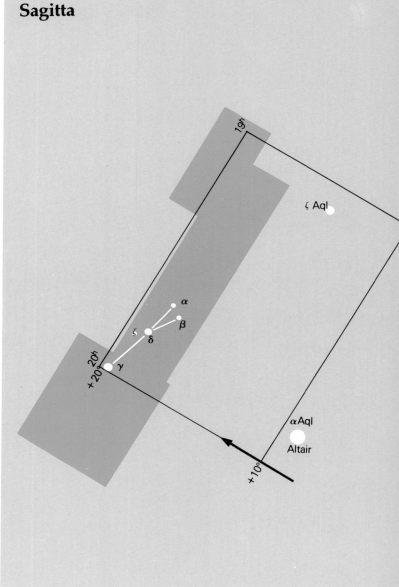

Pyxis Pyxidis Pyx *Compass*

Probably *the* most inconscpicuous of all the constellations, Pyxis was so named by Lacaille and appears insignificant beside the original Argo Navis constellation, now divided into Carina, Puppis and Vela. Pyxis is surrounded by Hydra, Puppis, Vela and Antlia and can be found between RA 8 hr 25 min–9 hrs 25 min and Dec – 17 – –37. It contains no stars of note.

Reticulum Reticuli Ret *Net*

Although usually included as one of the Lacaille constellations, Reticulum was defined earlier by a German called Habrecht. Rather than a net it actually represents a reticle, the grid of lines in the eyepiece of a telescope, used for defining stellar positions. It is easily located, north-west of the LMC. Only α Reticuli of mag 3·3, actually a double with component mags of 3·33 and 1·2, is of interest.

Sagitta Sagittae Sge *Arrow*

Sagitta was one of the Ptolemaic constellations, and lies across the Milky Way, north of Altair in Aquila. Sagitta contains only faint, uninteresting stars but it can be seen to possess a globular cluster, M71, approximately between stars γ and δ.

---- Ecliptic   ∘ variable star < mag. 5   ◇ planetary nebula
● double star   ◯ galaxy   ⊕ globular cluster
⊙ variable star > mag. 5   ◐ galactic nebula   ◌ open cluster

Sagittarius

Scorpius

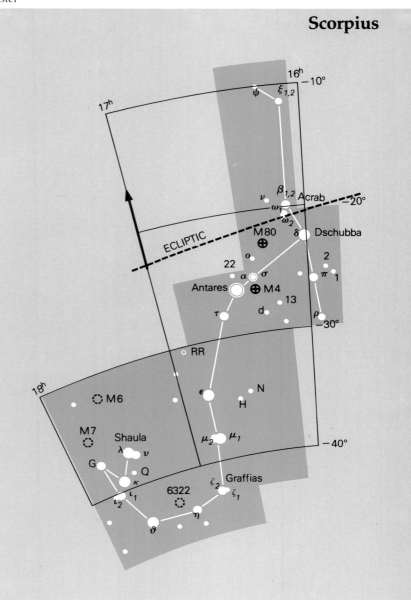

Sagittarius Sagittarii Sgr *Archer*

Of the 88 constellations, Sagittarius probably contains the most abundant and wide-ranging collection of objects. Within its area lie stars, the galactic nucleus, gaseous nebulae, open and galactic clusters – the list is virtually all embracing. It straddles the ecliptic and thus forms one of the zodiacal constellations.

The stars in Sagittarius receive Greek designations totally out of order with their measured apparent magnitude. The brightest star is ε, Kaus Australis, a mag 1·81 B9 type at 124 light years. Next is σ, Nunki, mag 2·12, a B2 star at 300 light years, followed by ζ, Ascella, a mag 2·61 of A2 spectrum, which is actually a double with mags 3·3 and 3·5. δ, Kaus Meridionalis, is less bright again of mag 2·71 with K2 spectrum and an absolute mag of 0·7, at a distance of 85 light years.

Star λ, Kaus Borealis is another K2, mag 2·8, at 71 light years distance, followed by γ, Al Nasl, of mag 2·97, a K0 type at 124 light years. Star η is actually a double with component mags of 3·17 and 10. A triple system, seen as star π Sagittarii, has mags of 3·7, 3·8 and 6·0. Elsewhere, the constellation displays the Trifid Nebula, M20, a faint and complex gas cloud, the Lagoon Nebula M8 and the Horse-shoe Nebula M17. Globular clusters M22, M28, M69, M70, M54, M55 and M75 are to be found as well as open clusters M18, M24, M25, M23 and M21.

Scorpius Scorpii Sco *Scorpion*

This is one of the zodiacal constellations, although the Sun only takes about a week to pass across it. The most interesting object by far is α, Antares, a supergiant variable (mag 0·86–1·02) with a distinctly green mag 6·5 companion. Antares has a diameter of about 563 million km with an M1 spectra and lies at a distance of 520 light years.

Star ε is a mag 2·28 K2 type at some 66 light years distance and stars δ, Dschubba, β, Graffias, τ, σ, π and μ are all B types within a range of mag 2·34–2·99, situated between 520 and 750 light years in distance. Other objects of interest in Scorpius include two globular clusters, M4 and M80, both of which are to be found fairly close to Antares. An open cluster, M6, is located within Scorpius as is M7, a much larger open cluster and one which is nearly lost in the great stellar clouds of the Milky Way. Large areas of the latter are seen across the southern sky and the central regions of this constellation.

Sculptor

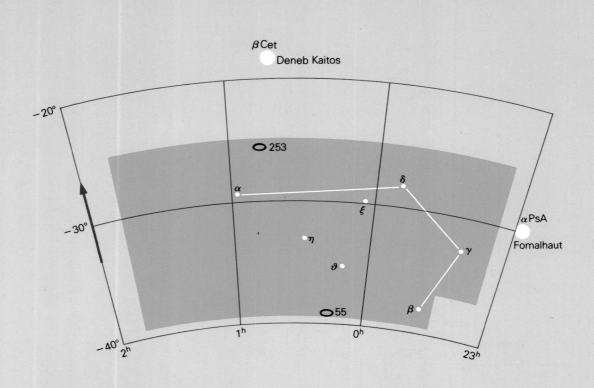

Scutum

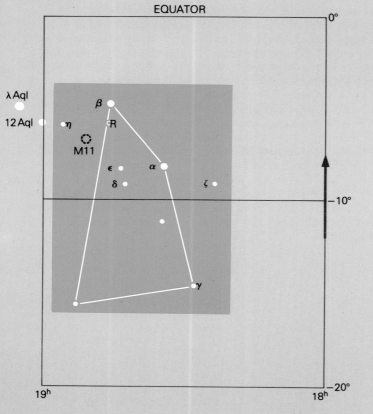

Sculptor Sculptoris Scl *Sculptor*

Sculptor was one of the Lacaille constellations, named in 1752, and lies to the east of Fomalhaut, α Piscis Austrini, from which it is best located. Sculptor contains the south galactic pole and few interesting stars. The most accurate position of the south galactic pole is on a point slightly north of a line drawn from star α to star ι. Little of note is contained in this constellation, although NGC 253 is a fairly bright external galaxy.

Scutum Scuti Sct *Shield*

A constellation named by Hevelius in 1690, Scutum is an inconspicuous patch of sky to the naked eye but a glorious crowded portion of the Milky Way through even a small telescope.

There are several stellar clusters, the most notable being M11 and M26. M11, the Wild Duck cluster, presents a very striking appearance. It probably contains over 600 stars in a region some 21 light years across, while its distance is about 6000 light years. R Scuti, just to the north-west, is an interesting binocular variable. δ Scuti is the prototype of a class of pulsating variable stars.

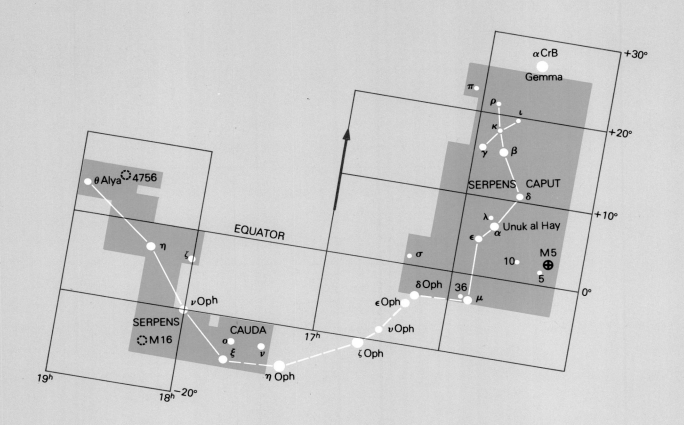

Serpens

Serpens Serpentis Ser *Serpent*
Serpens caput (serpent's head)
Serpens cauda (serpent's tail)

This constellation is divided into two: Serpens Caput and Serpens Cauda. It signifies the snake with which Ophiuchus is struggling and this certainly seems appropriate for the two halves are separated by that constellation.

The only prominent star here is α, Unuk al Hay, a mag 2·65 object. The remainder in Serpens Caput are faint but one of the brightest globular clusters, M5, is in this region. The brightest star in the other half of the constellation is ι, mag 3·4. M16 combines a star cluster and nebulosity, while NGC 4756 is a very scattered open cluster.

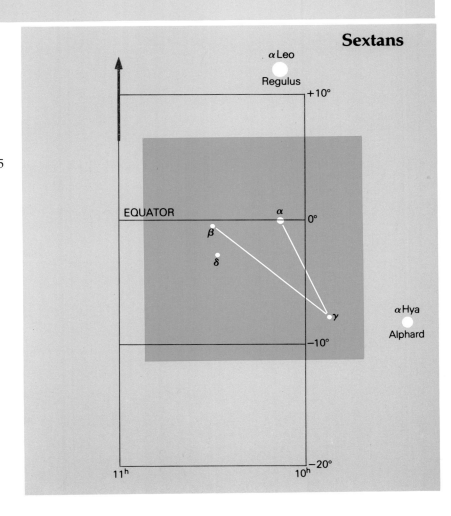

Sextans

Sextans Sextantis Sex *Sextant*

This constellation forms almost a perfect square and it is flanked by Leo, Hydra and Crater. The constellation was officially named by Hevelius in the late 17th century, but is uninteresting, containing only a few very faint doubles, variables and other objects.

Taurus

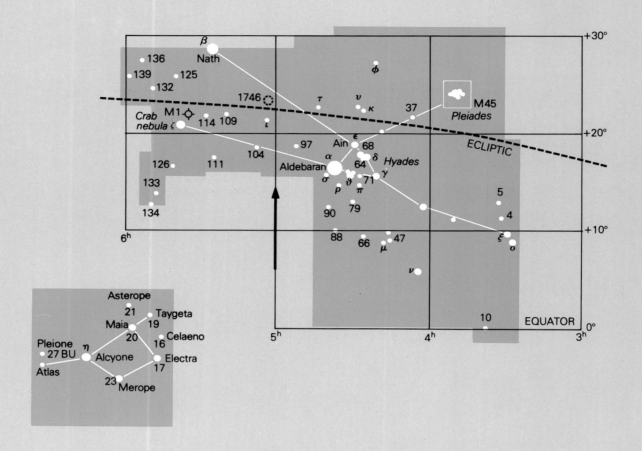

Taurus Tauri Tau *Bull*

Taurus the Bull was probably one of the first constellations to be named, and is reminiscent of the oldest domesticated animal. Prior to 3000 BC, Taurus lay across the vernal equinox. It is a remarkably rich area of the sky, containing some very prominent stars, the Pleiades and Hyades clusters, and the faint but very important Crab Nebula.

The most magnificent star, α, Aldebaran, is a K5 type giant with mag 0·86 and absolute mag −0·7 at a distance of 68 light years. It is a variable star with a diameter of about 50 million km and a luminosity 120 times that of the Sun. Star β, El Nath, is a mag 1·65 B7 type (absolute mag −3·2) at a distance of 300 light years.

Star η, Alcyone, is another B type with a mag of 2·86, as is star ζ with a mag of 3·07. These latter stars are 540 and 940 light years distant respectively. The Pleiades are found around Alcyone for that star is the most prominent member of this group, which actually consists of 300-odd stars. When viewed through the telescope, many hot blue stars, all very young, can be seen. Under favourable conditions some slight indications of the nebulosity, covering most of the area, may be visible. The system, with all parts moving through space together, is about 500 light years away.

Closer to Aldebaran the observer will find the Hyades, a cluster of nearer stars almost 130 light years away. Not far from ζ is the Crab Nebula, the remnant of a supernova that erupted in 1054 and which lies at a distance of 3500 light years.

Telescopium

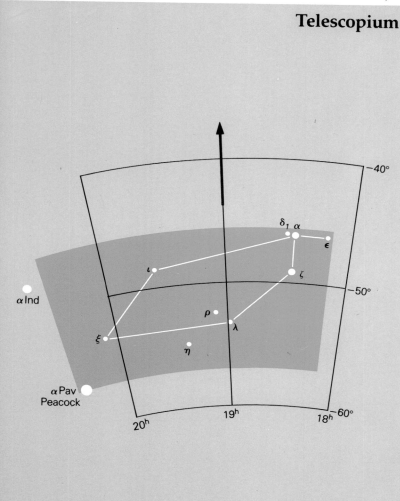

Triangulum

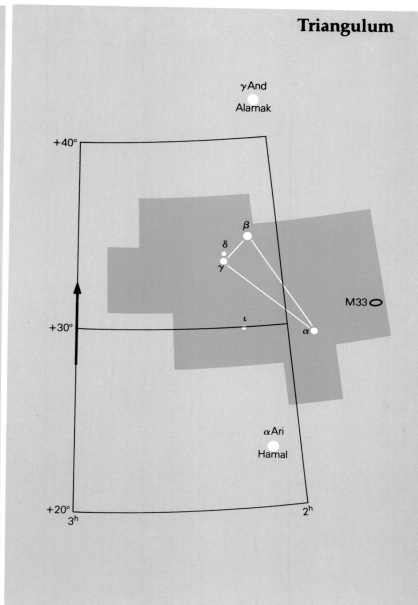

Telescopium Telescopii Tel *Telescope*

A constellation which should, perhaps, have been more properly included with Corona Australis. It is surrounded by that constellation and Ara, Pavo, Indus and Sagittarius. The three brightest stars are all nestled on the border with Corona Australis and there is little here of observational interest.

Triangulum Trianguli Tri *Triangle*

Triangulum is one of the earliest named constellations, despite being very inconspicuous. α Trianguli is only of mag 3·45 with β Trianguli of mag 3, which is again a departure from the correct sequence of decreasing magnitude for successive letter designations. The only object of note is the spiral galaxy M33, just visible to the naked eye under perfect conditions.

Key to constellations
scale of magnitude

0 1 2 3 4 5

Triangulum Australe

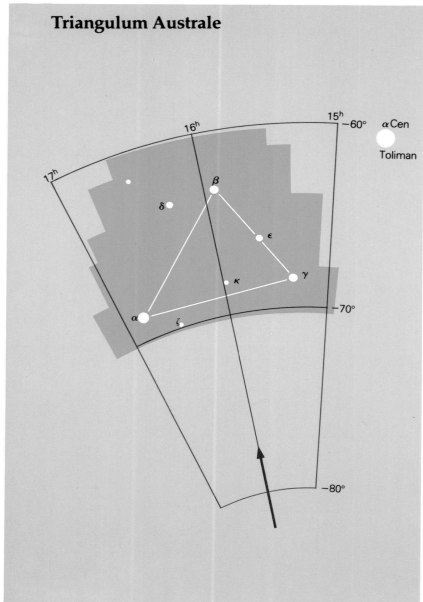

Tucana

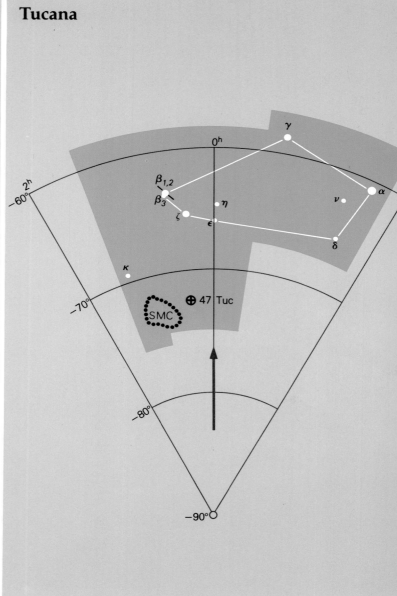

Triangulum Australe Trainguli Australis
TrA *Southern Triangle*

Triangulum Australe is a Bayer constellation listed in his early 17th-century catalogue. It is fairly easily found from α Centauris.

Star α is a mag 1·93 K2 type with absolute mag −0·1 at a distance of 82 light years; star β is a F2 type of mag 2·87 at 42 light years distance; and star γ is of mag 2·94 being an A0 type of absolute mag 0·2 at a distance 113 light years. Nothing else of note is found in this constellation.

Tucana Tucanae Tuc *Toucan*

Tucana contains most of the Small Magellanic Cloud (SMC). This irregular galaxy is close to our own and lies at a rather greater distance than the Large Magellanic Cloud in Dorado. The constellation contains several interesting nebulae and two globular clusters of which the most prominent is 47 Tuc, close to the SMC. Star α is a mag 2·8 K3 type at a distance of 62 light years.

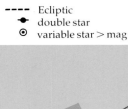

---- Ecliptic
◆ double star
⊙ variable star > mag. 5
∘ variable star < mag. 5
○ galaxy
◉ galactic nebula
◇ planetary nebula
⊕ globular cluster
◌ open cluster

Ursa Major

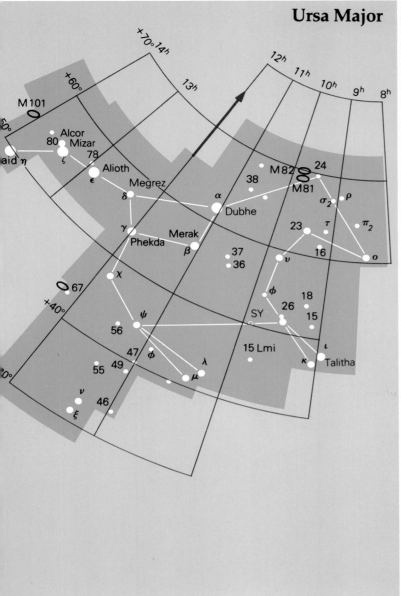

Ursa Minor

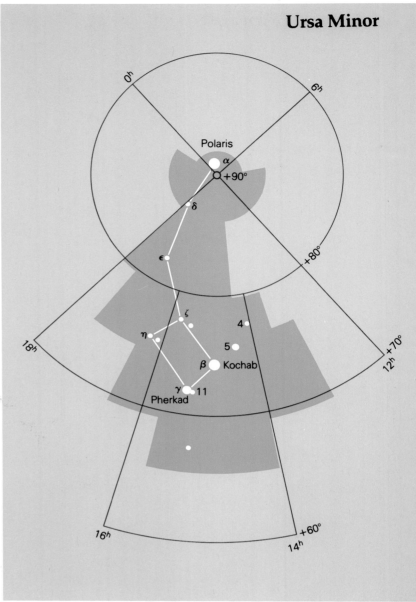

Ursa Major Ursae Majoris UMa *Great Bear*

This is possibly the most famous of all the constellations because its seven main stars are very prominent and easily visible from the northern hemisphere of the Earth. These seven stars, known as 'The Plough', 'The Wain' or 'The Big Dipper', only form a small part of the whole constellation. It has a highly irregular outline and prominent stars are spread across a large area.

Taking the Plough stars in sequence, and moving in increasing RA: α, Dubhe, is a mag 1·81 K0 close double with component mags of 1·88 and 4·82 and 107 light years away; star β, Merak, is a mag 2·37 A1 type with absolute mag 0·5 at a distance of 78 light years; γ, Phad, is an A0 type of mag 2·44 (absolute mag 0·2) 90 light years away; δ, Megrez, is a comparatively faint member at mag 3·3; ε, Alioth, is the brightest member of the seven at mag 1·79 with an A0 spectrum, absolute mag of 0·2 and it lies at a distance of 68 light years; star ζ, Mizar, is an A2 mag 2·06 double with component mags of 2·1 and 4·2 and the former is itself a double – the first spectroscopic binary to be discovered; and finally, η, Alkaid, at the comparatively remote distance of 210 light years, is a B3 type of mag 1·87 (absolute mag −2·1).

Four interesting doubles are located in the constellation: star θ is actually a double with mag 3·19 and 14: star ι has mag 3·12 and 10·8 components: star $\varkappa$ has component mags of 4·0 and 4·2; and star o, Muscida, has components of mag 3·57 and 15. There are six Messier objects in the constellation (M81, M82, M97, M101, M108 and M109). M97 is the famous planetary Owl Nebula, looking like a staring owl, with the remainder being galaxies in their own right.

Ursa Minor Ursae Minoris UMi *Little Bear*

Ura Minor was one of the originally named 48 constellations, and has the distinction of including the north celestial pole. Much of Ursa Minor seems nestled within the cradle of Draco but this constellation is unmistakably distinctive and having found the star nearest to the north celestial pole the rest is easy to recognize.

The pole star itself, or the star which today is closest to the north celestial pole, is Polaris, α UMi, a mag 1·99–2·1 variable of F8 type and an absolute mag of −4·6. Lying at a distance of 680 light years, the star is attended by a mag 8·9 companion. Star β, Kochab, is a mag 2·04 K4 type and star γ, Pherkad, is of mag 2·04 so that when Polaris, a notable Cepheid, is dim it is actually slightly fainter than these stars.

Constellation maps

Vela

Key to constellations
scale of magnitude
0 1 2 3 4 5

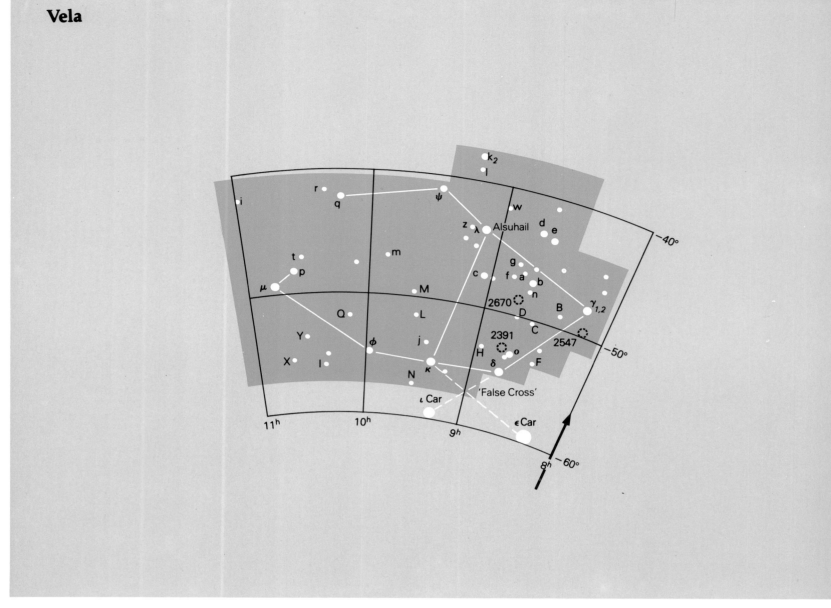

Vela *Velorum* Vel *Sail (of a ship)*

Vela is one of the three constellations formed from the
original, and unwieldy, Argo Navis. It is bordered by Antila,
Pyxis, Puppis, Carina and Centaurus. The designation of the
various stars was set up when Vela was part of Argo Navis
and the brightest star here is γ Velorum, a double with
component mags of 2·2 and 4·8. Star δ, is a mag 1·95 A0 type
with a mag 5·1 companion. A third companion to δ is actually
a spectroscopic binary viewed as a single mag 10 star. The
stars δ and κ, together with ι and ε in Carina form the 'False
Cross', sometimes mistaken for the constellation of Crux.

Virgo

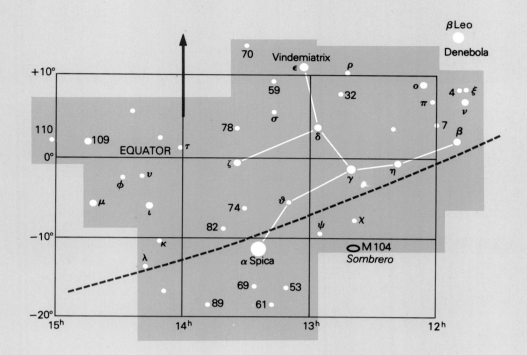

Virgo Virginis Vir *Virgin*

Virgo is a zodiacal constellation and is second only to Hydra in area.

The most prominent star in the constellation is α, Spica, southernmost of the seven brightest stars, with mag 0·91 and a location 220 light years from the Sun. The star is a variable with a mag 1·01 companion and is seen as a hot white object. Star γ, 2·76 and an absolute mag of $-3·3$ is a close binary with a combined magnitude of 2·76 and an absolute mag of $-3·3$. It lies at a distance of only 32 light years. Far to the west of the constellation lies β, Zavijava, of mag 3·8, and to the north ε, Vindemiatrix, is a mag 2·86 star of spectral type G9 with an absolute mag of 0·6 at a distance of 90 light years.

Virgo lies adjacent to Coma Berenices and the northern border of Virgo contains many interesting nebulae – all external galaxies. Most notable are M58, M59, M60, M84, M87, M89 and M90. On the south-western border (with Corvus) the telescope will reveal the magnificent Sombrero Galaxy (M104), M49 and M61 lie between stars β and ε.

Constellation maps

Key to constellations
scale of magnitude
0 1 2 3 4 5

Volans

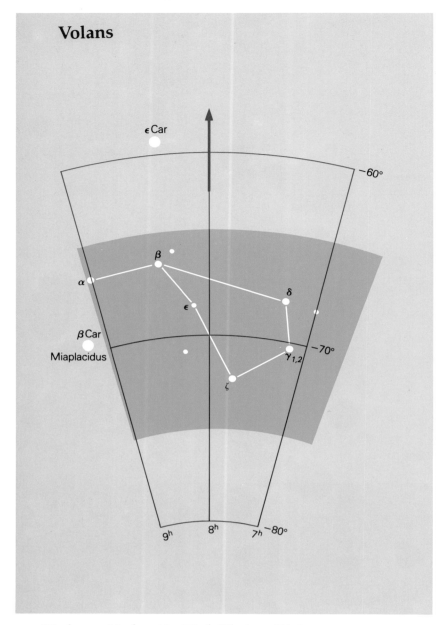

Vulpecula

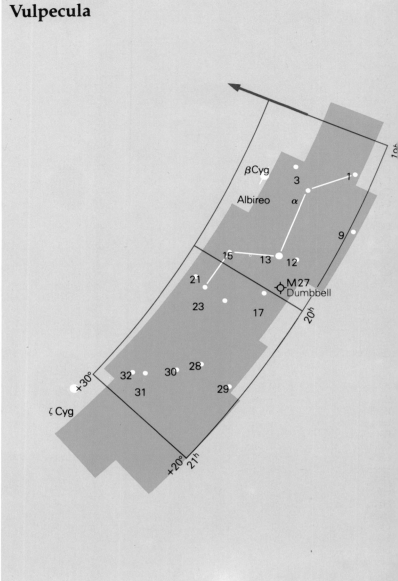

Volans Volantis Vol *Flying Fish*

One of Bayer's constellations, Volans is more properly seen as an adjunct to Carina as it is most easily found from the stars β and ε Carinae. None of the stars in this region of the celestial sphere is of significance or as bright as mag 3. The keen observer may be able to discern the mag 9 companion to ζ and, far more easily, make out the K1 and G0 components of the double star γ.

Vulpecula Vulpeculae Vul *Little Fox*

Vulpecula was one of the constellations named by Hevelius in 1690 and is situated alongside Sagitta but is probably best located from the star Albireo, β Cygni.

The constellation lies across part of the Milky Way, including an extension of the 'Great Rift' in Cygnus. The stars within Vulpecula are very faint and extremely inconspicuous and there is nothing of very great note in the constellation. The nebula M27 (NGC 6853) can be found to the south, close to the border with Sagitta. This is a planetary nebula and is widely known as the Dumbbell.

The constellations

Latin Name	Genitive	Abbreviation	Translation	Right Ascension (h)	Declination (degrees)	Area occupied (square degrees)
Andromeda	Andromedae	And	Andromeda	1	+40	772
Antlia	Antliae	Ant	Pump	10	−35	239
Apus	Apodis	Aps	Bird of Paradise	16	−75	206
Aquarius	Aquarii	Aqr	Water Bearer	23	−15	980
Aquila	Aquilae	Aql	Eagle	20	+ 5	652
Ara	Arae	Ara	Altar	17	−55	237
Aries	Arietis	Ari	Ram	3	+20	441
Auriga	Aurigae	Aur	Charioteer	6	+40	657
Boötes	Boötis	Boo	Herdsman	15	+30	907
Caelum	Caeli	Cae	Chisel	5	−40	125
Camelopardalis	Camelopardalis	Cam	Giraffe	6	+70	757
Cancer	Cancri	Cnc	Crab	9	+20	506
Canes Venatici	Canum Venaticorum	CVn	Hunting Dogs	13	+40	465
Canis Major	Canis Majoris	CMa	Big Dog	7	+20	380
Canis Minor	Canis Minoris	CMi	Little Dog	8	+ 5	183
Capricornus	Capricorni	Cap	Sea Goat	21	−20	414
Carina	Carinae	Car	Keel (of a ship)	9	−60	494
Cassiopeia	Cassiopeiae	Cas	Cassiopeia	1	+60	598
Centaurus	Centauri	Cen	Centaur	13	−50	1060
Cepheus	Cephei	Cep	Cepheus	22	+70	588
Cetus	Ceti	Cet	Whale	2	−10	1231
Chamaeleon	Chamaeleontis	Cha	Chameleon	11	−80	132
Circinus	Circini	Cir	Compass	15	−60	93
Columba	Columbae	Col	Dove	6	−35	270
Coma Berenices	Comae Berenices	Com	Berenice's Hair	13	+20	386
Corona Australis	Coronae Australis	CrA	Southern Crown	19	−40	128
Corona Borealis	Coronae Borealis	CrB	Northern Crown	16	+30	179
Corvus	Corvi	Crv	Crow	12	−20	184
Crater	Crateris	Crt	Cup	11	−15	282
Crux	Crucis	Cru	Cross	12	−60	68
Cygnus	Cygni	Cyg	Swan	21	+40	804
Delphinus	Delphini	Del	Dolphin	21	+10	189
Dorado	Doradus	Dor	Dorado	5	−65	179
Draco	Draconis	Dra	Dragon	17	+65	1083
Equuleus	Equulei	Equ	Little Horse	21	+10	72
Eridanus	Eridani	Eri	River Eridanus	3	−20	1138
Fornax	Fornacis	For	Furnace	3	−30	398
Gemini	Geminorum	Gem	Twins	7	+20	514
Grus	Gruis	Gru	Crane	22	−45	366
Hercules	Herculis	Her	Hercules	17	+30	1225
Horologium	Horologii	Hor	Clock	3	−60	249
Hydra	Hydrae	Hya	Hydra (water monster)	10	−20	1303
Hydrus	Hydri	Hyi	Sea serpent	2	−75	243
Indus	Indi	Ind	Indian	21	−55	294
Lacerta	Lacertae	Lac	Lizard	22	+45	201
Leo	Leonis	Leo	Lion	11	+15	947
Leo Minor	Leonis Minoris	LMi	Little Lion	10	+35	232
Lepus	Leporis	Lep	Hare	6	−20	290
Libra	Librae	Lib	Scales	15	−15	538
Lupus	Lupi	Lup	Wolf	15	−45	334
Lynx	Lyncis	Lyn	Lynx	8	+45	545
Lyra	Lyrae	Lyr	Lyre	19	+40	286
Mensa	Mensae	Men	Table (Mountain)	5	−80	153
Microscopium	Microscopii	Mic	Microscope	21	−35	210
Monoceros	Monocerotis	Mon	Unicorn	7	− 5	482
Musca	Muscae	Mus	Fly	12	−70	138
Norma	Normae	Nor	Level (square)	16	−50	165
Octans	Octantis	Oct	Octant	22	−85	291
Ophiuchus	Ophiuchi	Oph	Ophiuchus (serpent bearer)	17	0	948
Orion	Orionis	Ori	Orion	5	+ 5	594
Pavo	Pavonis	Pav	Peacock	20	−65	378
Pegasus	Pegasi	Peg	Pegasus (winged horse)	22	+20	1121
Perseus	Persei	Per	Perseus	3	+45	615
Phoenix	Phoenicis	Phe	Phoenix	1	−50	469
Pictor	Pictoris	Pic	Easel	6	−55	247
Pisces	Piscium	Psc	Fishes	1	+15	889
Piscis Austrinus	Piscis Austrini	PsA	Southern Fish	22	−30	245
Puppis	Puppis	Pup	Stern (of a ship)	8	−40	673
Pyxis	Pyxidis	Pyx	Compass	9	−30	221
Reticulum	Reticuli	Ret	Net	4	−60	114
Sagitta	Sagittae	Sge	Arrow	20	+10	80
Sagittarius	Sagittarii	Sgr	Archer	19	−25	867
Scorpius	Scorpii	Sco	Scorpion	17	−40	497
Sculptor	Sculptoris	Scl	Sculptor	0	−30	475
Scutum	Scuti	Sct	Shield	19	−10	109
Serpens	Sepentis	Ser	Serpent			
Serpens caput			Serpent's head	16	+10	429
Serpens cauda			Serpent's tail	18	− 5	208
Sextans	Sextantis	Sex	Sextant	10	0	314
Taurus	Tauri	Tau	Bull	4	+15	797
Telescopium	Telescopii	Tel	Telescope	19	−50	252
Triangulum	Trainguli	Tri	Triangle	2	+30	132
Triangulum Australe	Trianguli Australis	TrA	Southern Triangle	16	−65	110
Tucana	Tucanae	Tuc	Toucan	0	−65	295
Ursa Major	Ursae Majoris	UMa	Great Bear	11	+50	1280
Ursa Minor	Ursae Minoris	UMi	Little Bear	15	+70	256
Vela	Velorum	Vel	Sails (of a ship)	9	−50	500
Virgo	Virginis	Vir	Virgin	13	0	1294
Volans	Volantis	Vol	Flying Fish	8	−70	141
Vulpecula	Vulpeculae	Vul	Little Fox	20	+25	268

The Sun

Never look directly at the Sun with any form of equipment, or even just the naked eye. Blindness or lasting damage may result. Even when the Sun is low on the horizon harmful amounts of infrared radiation can still reach the eye. Moreover, so-called 'Sun' filters, supplied with some small telescopes, are not safe, so do not use them. The only method of observation that can be recommended is to project an image onto a suitable screen. This may be either a card held behind the eyepiece of the telescope (preferably with a screen to shade it from other light) or else a simple five-sided box. Make sure that any finder is covered – or the second objective lens if you are using binoculars – with a tight-fitting cap. Do not allow the telescope to point at the Sun for too long as it may also be damaged by the concentrated heat. There are several other methods that may be used to observe the Sun in safety, but none are as simple as the projection method.

The brilliant surface of the Sun is known as the photosphere and has a temperature of about 6000 K. Its most noticeable features are sunspots, darker (and cooler) areas that usually show a dark centre (the umbra) and a lighter surrounding region (the penumbra). Sunspot numbers change with the 11-year sunspot cycle, and occasionally there may be none visible on the disk. They frequently appear in pairs (actually linked by magnetic fields) and active areas may consist of many individual sunspots. The solar rotation – which is faster at the equator that at the poles – carries the features across the disk from day to day. Although most individual spots do not last long, some may persist for more than one solar rotation (about 27 days), especially if they form part of a large active area. The numbers of sunspots and active areas can be followed easily by projection methods. During the sunspot cycle the main centres of activity gradually migrate towards the equator, before beginning again at high latitudes.

Under good conditions tiny features, known as granulation, may be seen on the solar surface, together with larger bright areas (faculae), more easily seen towards the limbs. During a total solar eclipse large, glowing prominences may be visible around the limb where material is moving towards, or away from, the surface. With specialized equipment these prominences may be seen outside eclipses, and also as dark features above the central regions of the disk, when they are known as filaments. Occasionally brilliant flares may erupt, actually just above the photosphere, and disturb neighbouring filaments as well as ejecting sprays of particles out into space.

The Sun's outer atmosphere (the corona) is also visible during an eclipse. Its density is very low, but the gases are extremely hot (around 2 million K). When the Sun is completely covered by the Moon plumes and rays may frequently be seen extending far out into space.

The two main spots in this group clearly show the umbral and penumbral regions, as well as 'bridges' across the central areas.

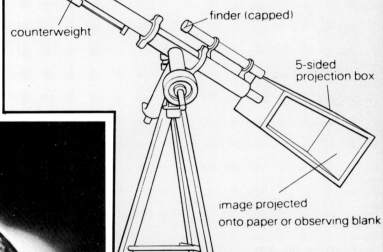

An observing box is the most convenient way of safely studying the image of the Sun, and of projecting the image onto a blank for drawing.

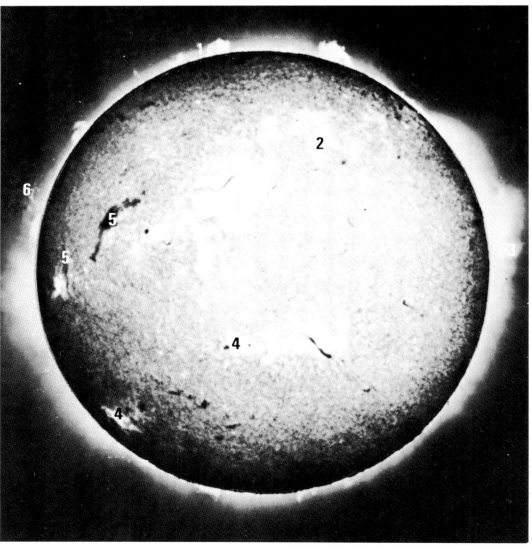

A composite of a photograph taken in the Hα line of ionized hydrogen, superimposed on a white-light photograph of the corona. Faculae in white light are similar to plages (shown here).

1 *quiescent prominence*
2 *hydrogen – α plage*
3 *coronal plumes*
4 *sunspot groups*
5 *filaments*
6 *active prominence*

Aurorae

Aurorae are generally visible to observers at fairly high latitudes – beyond about 50° N and S – but on rare occasions they do occur right down towards the equator. The numbers of aurorae that are seen vary with the general cycle of solar activity, most aurorae occurring perhaps a year or two after sunspot maximum. Some auroral activity may occur at more or less any time, but the most brilliant displays come when there has been violent activity on the Sun. Energetic solar flares eject streams of charged particles into space as part of the solar wind. These interact with the region governed by the Earth's magnetic field (the magnetosphere) and give rise to showers of energetic particles that follow the magnetic field lines down towards the surface. In the high atmosphere between about 100–300 km (or occasionally even as high as 1000 km) these excite atoms of gases, which emit light and thus give rise to the auroral displays. These occur most frequently in two 'ovals' around the Earth's a magnetic poles. At times of great solar activity these ovals expand in size, and the auroral displays tend to move down to lower latitudes.

Displays take many forms, but usually begin quietly, build up to maximum intensity around local midnight and then fade away towards dawn. The pattern partly depends upon the observing site, and maxium activity is often in the early hours of the morning, although some positions regularly find that the displays are over by midnight. Some displays are highly active, altering with each passing moment and moving rapidly around the sky. Others evolve very slowly, or just brighten slightly and then fade away.

One of the most common forms of display is the arc (A) which may stretch smoothly across the sky. Another shows 'folds' like a curtain, and is known as a band (B). Arcs and bands always have smooth lower edges. An ill-defined bright area, often mistaken for a cloud, is called a patch (P) and individual shafts of light stretching upwards in the sky are rays (R). The terms 'homogeneous' (H) and 'rayed' (R) are used to describe in more detail the appearance of the various forms. Homogeneous arcs (HA) are very commonly encountered, for example. Throughout a display the forms may change from one type to another and there may be surges in brightness, and alterations in the colours.

The appearance of a display largely depends upon the position of the observer, although the region that is covered may also shift north or south during the course of a night. Sometimes only a glow may be visible along the horizon towards the magnetic pole, or else just the tops of a few high rays may appear. Closer to the display, single or multiple arcs or bands may be apparent across a large portion of the sky. On other occasions the display may take place right overhead. In such a coronal display (C) shafts of light may appear to converge on the zenith from all round the horizon.

Above *An active homogeneous arc (HA), with sharp lower edge and diffuse upper border, photographed from Scotland. The different colours arise from various oxygen emissions.*

Above right *A quiet homogeneous band (HB), showing the characteristic smooth lower border and curtain-like fold. Photographed in Canada in front of the rising constellation of Taurus.*

Below *Active, multiple rayed bands (RB), which were continually altering in shape and strength, illustrate some of the complexity seen in major displays.*

Below right *A corona (C) photographed above Auriga from Skibotn, Norway. The classic converging fan-shaped appearance of the rays is noticeable.*

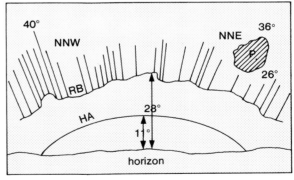

The positions of auroral features are described by their angular distances from the horizon together with their compass directions.

RB = Rayed Band
HA = Homogeneous Art
P = Patch

Eclipses of the Sun and Moon

Lunar and solar eclipses are infrequent because the orbit of the Moon is inclined to the plane of the ecliptic (the Earth's orbit around the Sun). The average angle between the orbits is about 5°, but this varies considerably. Eclipses can obviously occur only at New or Full Moon when the three bodies are more or less in line, but on most occasions the Moon is above or below the ecliptic. Only when the Moon crosses a node – one of the two points where the orbital planes intersect – at the right time is an eclipse produced.

The changing apparent size of the Moon is particularly important in a solar eclipse. When the Moon is closest to the Earth (at perigee) it may completely cover the Sun, giving a total eclipse. This can never last longer than 7 minutes 40 seconds, but is usually much less. On the other hand, in an annular eclipse, the Moon is most distant (close to apogee) and the dark inner shadow (the umbra) does not reach the surface of the Earth, so that a ring of light remains visible around the Moon. Even under the most favourable conditions the maximum width of the path of totality across the surface of the Earth is only about 270 km. The track where annular eclipses can be seen is even narrower. Depending on the circumstances, the path of the eclipse may begin and end as

annular, with a short total portion in the middle, where the Moon's umbra touches the Earth. Outside the central track, a partial eclipse may be seen over a much wider area.

Solar eclipses occur between two and five times a year, but can be seen from such a restricted area that more than 300 years elapse before another one is visible from the same place on Earth. Lunar eclipses are less frequent (two or three each year), but much easier to see, as they are visible from the whole of the hemisphere where the Moon is above the horizon. When the Moon passes through the Earth's outer shadow (the penumbra) the change in brightness is so low that it is not noticeable to the naked eye. In partial or total lunar eclipses the difference is marked. The Earth's atmosphere absorbs blue light and refracts the remainder towards the centre of the umbra, where the Moon appears dimly illuminated by red light. A bluish fringe is usually visible around the edge of the umbra. Some of the brighter features may remain visible throughout the eclipse. The change in the Moon's distance also plays a part, as when at perigee (closest) it passes further into the darkest central region of the umbra.

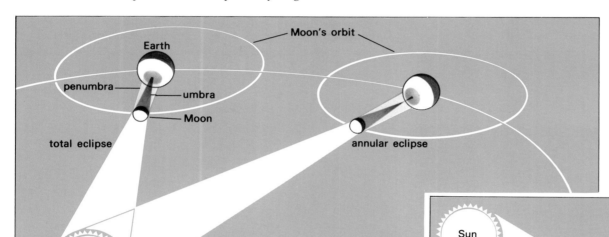

Total (left) *and annular eclipses of the Sun. Although shown in the same plane as the orbit of the Earth for the sake of simplicity, the Moon's orbit actually varies in its inclination, as well as swinging round the Earth in a complex manner.*

Although the Earth casts a very large penumbral cone of shadow (not shown here) a lunar eclipse is only noticeable when the Moon is within the dark umbra.

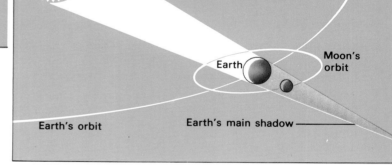

Solar Eclipses 1984–1999

Date	Type of Eclipse	Maximum Duration	Track
1984 Nov. 22–23	Total	1m 59s	E. Indies, S. Pacific
1985 May 19	Partial		Arctic
1985 Nov. 12	Total	1m 55s	S. Pacific, Antarctica
1986 Apr. 9	Partial		Antarctic
1986 Oct. 3	Annular/Total	0m 1s	N. Atlantic
1987 Mar. 29	Annular/Total	0m 56s	Argentina, Atlantic, Congo, Indian Ocean
1987 Sept. 23	Annular		USSR, China, Pacific
1988 Mar. 11	Total	3m 46s	Indian Ocean, E. Indies, Pacific
1988 Sept. 11	Annular		Indian Ocean, S. of Australia, Antarctic
1989 Mar. 7	Partial		Arctic
1989 Aug. 31	Partial		Antarctic
1990 Jan. 26	Annular		Antarctica
1990 July 22	Total	2m 33s	Finland, USSR, Pacific
1991 Jan. 15–16	Annular		Australia, New Zealand, Pacific
1991 July 11	Total	6m 54s	Pacific, Central America, Brazil
1992 Jan. 4–5	Annular		Central Pacific
1992 Dec. 24	Partial		Arctic
1993 May 21	Partial		Arctic
1994 May 10	Annular		Pacific, Mexico, USA, Canada, Atlantic
1994 Nov. 3	Total	4m 23s	Peru, Brazil, S. Atlantic
1995 Apr. 29	Annular		S. Pacific, Peru, Brazil, S. Atlantic
1995 Oct. 24	Total	2m 5s	Iran, India, E. Indies, Pacific
1996 Apr. 17	Partial		Antarctic
1996 Oct. 12	Partial		Arctic
1997 Mar. 9	Total	2m 50s	USSR, Arctic
1997 Sept. 2	Partial		Antarctic
1998 Feb. 26	Total	3m 56s	Pacific, S. of Panama, Atlantic
1998 Aug 22	Annular		Indian Ocean, E. Indies, Pacific
1999 Feb. 16	Annular		Indian Ocean, Australia, Pacific
1999 Aug 11	Total	2m 23s	Atlantic, England, France, Central Europe, Turkey, India

Lunar Eclipses 1984–2000

Date	Type of Eclipse	Duration	Region of visibility
1985 May 4	Total	70m	Europe, Africa, Asia, Australia
1985 Oct. 28	Total	42m	Europe, Africa, Asia, Australia
1986 Apr. 24	Total	68m	E. Asia, Australia, Antarctic
1986 Oct. 17	Total	74m	Asia, Europe, Africa, Australia
1987 Oct. 7	Partial	–	–
1988 Mar. 3	Partial	–	E. Europe, E. Africa, Asia, Australia
1988 Aug. 27	Partial	–	E. Asia, Australia, Antarctic, N. America
1989 Feb. 20	Total	76m	Europe, Asia, Australia, N. America
1989 Aug. 17	Total	98m	N. & S. America, Europe, Africa
1990 Feb. 9	Total	46m	E. Atlantic, Europe, Africa, Asia, Australia
1990 Aug. 6	Partial	–	Australia, Asia, Antarctic
1991 Dec. 21	Partial	–	Asia, N. Australia, N. America
1992 June 15	Partial	–	N. & S America, Antarctic, W. Africa
1992 Dec. 10.	Total	74m	N. & S. America, Europe, Africa, W. Asia
1993 June 4	Total	98m	E. Asia, Australia, Antarctic
1993 Nov. 29	Total	50m	N. & S. America, W. Europe, NE. Asia.
1994 May 25	Partial	–	N. & S. America, W. Europe, Africa
1995 Apr. 15	Partial	–	E. Asia, Australia, Pacific, N. America
1996 Apr. 4	Total	84m	N. & S. America, Europe, Africa, W. Asia
1996 Sept. 27	Total	72m	N. & S. America, Europe, Africa
1997 Mar. 24	Partial	–	N. & S. America, W. Europe, W. Africa
1997 Sept. 16	Total	66m	Europe, Africa, Asia, Australia, Antarctic
1998 (no eclipses)			
1999 July 28	Partial	–	E. Asia, Australia, Pacific, N. America
2000 Jan. 21	Total	84m	N. & S. America, Europe, W. Africa
2000 July 16	Total	102m	E. Asia, Australia, Antarctic

The Moon

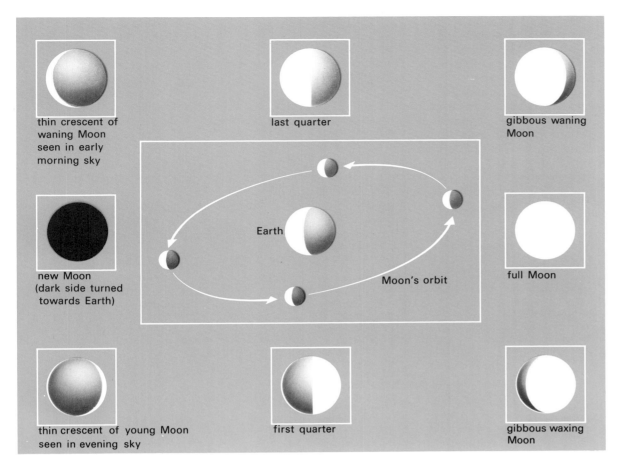

thin crescent of waning Moon seen in early morning sky

last quarter

gibbous waning Moon

new Moon (dark side turned towards Earth)

Earth

Moon's orbit

full Moon

thin crescent of young Moon seen in evening sky

first quarter

gibbous waxing Moon

The moon turns the same face towards the Earth throughout its orbit, which it completes once a month (29·5 days). Most lunar features are best seen twice in that time, when they are close to the terminator (the line dividing the illuminated and dark portions), at sunrise and sunset. In the small crescent phases some details in the dark region may be seen by light reflected from the Earth ('Earthshine'). At full Moon the bright ray systems become very prominent.

Below left The Montes Apenninus form part of the rim of the Mare Imbrium basin. The floor of Archimedes has been flooded with mare lavas.

Below Copernicus shows terraced interior walls, a central peak, secondary craters outside the rim, and a bright ray system.

Most of the bright highland area of the Moon is 'saturated' with craters, produced by meteoritic impacts. Small craters such as Birt (165 on map overleaf) have fairly smooth interiors, but larger ones have flat floors (Davy 169) or central peaks (Agrippa 44). The largest, such as Bailly (152), more than 300 km across, are very shallow, frequently only 2–4 km deep. They usually show complex walls with internal terraces, multiple central peaks (Langrenus 245) and secondary craters outside the rim (Copernicus 96). Some have notably flat floors (Ptolemaeus 170), while others are strongly rifted (Gassendi 123, Petavius 238). There are many overlapping craters, some forming crater chains, such as Vallis Rheita near Rheita itself (218). Thebit (164) has a perfect smaller crater on its main wall. Comparatively recent impacts threw out ejecta and gave rise to the bright ray systems, most notably those of Tycho (156) and Copernicus (96). Some individual craters such as Aristarchus (81) are very bright and prominent.

The prominent dark maria ('seas') were formed by flows of fluid lava. Circular maria, such as Mare Crisium, are directly related to giant impact basins. Mare Imbrium is similar, and the surrounding mountain ranges (including Montes Apenninus and Montes Alpes) are part of the original crater's rim. Other peaks, such as Piton (74) and Pico (75) project above the surface of the lava. The ejecta from this impact 'sculptured' much of the surface, well beyond Mare Vaporum and Sinus Medii. The irregular maria such as Mare Vaporum, Mare Spumans and Palus Epidemiarum are not related to individual impacts, but arose when thin lava flows covered irregular, low-lying areas.

Craters that have been flooded by lava have perfectly flat floors (Archimedes 85), some notably dark (Plato 76, Grimaldi 114, Billy 116). Many others have been partly destroyed by mare lavas. Sinus Iridum is the best example; others are Fracastorius (221), Le Monnier (27) and Letronne (115). Some old craters were buried, forming 'ghost' craters such as Stadius (95) and those near Arago (36) and Lambert (87). Low illumination is needed to see these rings and mare wrinkle ridges, such as those in Mare Serenitatis and Oceanus Procellarum.

The central region of the disk has many clefts (rimae), with systems around Triesnecker (46) and Hyginus (48), and the long Rima Ariadaeus. A rift breaks the walls of Goclenius

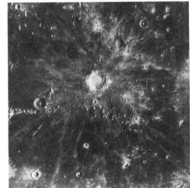

Lavas have covered the circular Mare Serenitatis and also the irregular area, Lacus Somniorum (bottom left). The one prominent crater is Posidonius.

Mare Nubium with Rupes Recta '('the Straight Wall'). The Moon's heavily cratered highlands lie to the north and east. The three prominent craters are Alphonsus, Arzachel and Ptolomaeus.

(241) and continues far into Mare Foecunditatis. Many others exist around the borders of Mare Humorum. Nearby Mare Nubium contains Rupes Recta, a fault close to the crater Birt (165). The long Rupes Altai is probably an old scarp, altered by later cratering. Sinuous rilles such as the striking Vallis Schröteri (93) and the one in the floor of Vallis Alpes are the remains of collapsed lava tubes.

The Moon map

Most major features are shown on this map as well as a few important smaller ones. The international (Latin) names are used throughout. Some features are slightly emphasized to help with identification, but visibility varies greatly with the elevation of the Sun, and even prominent craters may disappear under high sunlight. Various effects (known as libration) cause the Moon to appear to sway backwards and forwards, so all features change slightly in shape and position relative to the centre of the disk. Some regions near the limb (the apparent edge), may only be seen clearly at long intervals.

1 Neper
2 Apollonius
3 Firmicius
4 Condorcet
5 Taruntius
6 Picard
7 Proclus
8 Macrobius
9 Cleomedes
10 Hahn
11 Berosus
12 Gauss
13 Burckhardt
14 Geminus
15 Messala
16 Mercurius
17 Franklin
18 Cepheus
19 Oersted
20 Atlas
21 Hercules
22 Endymion
23 De La Rue
24 Vitruvius
25 Promontorium Argaeus
26 Littrow
27 Le Monnier
28 Chacornac
29 Posidonius
30 Mason
31 Plana
32 Bürg
33 Maskelyne
34 Sabine
35 Ritter
36 Arago
37 Julius Caesar
38 Plinius
39 Promontorium Acherusia
40 Menaelaus
41 Bessel
42 Linné
43 Godin
44 Agrippa
45 Rhaeticus
46 Triesnecker
47 Pallas
48 Hyginus
49 Boscovich
50 Manilius
51 Conon
52 Autolycus
53 Aristillus
54 Theatetus
55 Cassini
56 Callipus
57 Alexander
58 Eudoxus
59 Aristoteles
60 Gärtner
61 Arnold
62 Meton
63 W. Bond
64 Barrow
65 Goldschmidt
66 Anaxagoras
67 Philolaus
68 Anaximenes
69 Carpenter
70 J. Herschel
71 Pythagoras
72 Babbage
73 Harpalus
74 Mons Piton
75 Mons Pico
76 Plato
77 Le Verrier
78 Helicon

79 Promontorium Laplace
80 Bianchini
81 Sharp
82 Promontorium Heraclides
83 Mairan
84 Mons Rümker
85 Archimedes
86 Timocharis
87 Lambert
88 Euler
89 Delisle
90 Prinz
91 Aristarchus
92 Herodotus
93 Vallis Schröteri
94 Eratosthenes
95 Stadius
96 Copernicus
97 Gay Lussac
98 Mayer
99 Gambart
100 Reinhold
101 Landsberg
102 Encke
103 Kepler
104 Marius
105 Reiner
106 Otto Struve
107 Seleucus
108 Krafft
109 Cardanus
110 Cavalerius
111 Hevelius
112 Hedin
113 Riccioli
114 Grimaldi
115 Letronne
116 Billy
117 Hansteen
118 Sirsalis
119 Rocca
120 Crüger
121 Darwin
122 Byrgius
123 Gassendi
124 Mersenius
125 Cavendish
126 Vieta
127 Lagrange
128 Piazzi
129 Agatharchides
130 Bullialdus
131 Kies
132 Mercator
133 Campanus
134 Vitello
135 Hesiodus
136 Pitatus
137 Gauricus
138 Würzelbauer
139 Cichus
140 Capuanus
141 Heinsius
142 Wilhelm
143 Mee
144 Schickard
145 Wargentin
146 Phocylides
147 Schiller
148 Longomontanus
149 Clavius
150 Blancanus
151 Scheiner
152 Bailly
153 Curtius
154 Moretus
155 Maginus
156 Tycho

157 Saussure
158 Orontius
159 Nasireddin
160 Lexell
161 Walter
162 Regiomontanus
163 Purbach
164 Thebit
165 Birt
166 Arzachel
167 Alpetragius
168 Alphonsus
169 Davy
170 Ptolomaeus
171 W. Herschel
172 Flammarion
173 Mösting
174 Guericke
175 Parry
176 Bonpland
177 Fra Mauro
178 Manilius
179 Jacobi
180 Cuvier
181 Licetus
182 Stöfler
183 Faraday
184 Aliacensis
185 Werner
186 Blanchinus
187 Lacaille
188 Apianus
189 Playfair
190 Airy
191 Argelander
192 Albategnius
193 Klein
194 Hipparchus
195 Vlacq
196 Hommel
197 Pitiscus
198 Baco
199 Barocius
200 Maurolycus
201 Buch
202 Büsching
203 Riccius
204 Rabbi Levi
205 Zagut
206 Pontanus
207 Sacrobosco
208 Azophi
209 Abenezra
210 Geber
211 Tacitus
212 Almanon
213 Abulfeda
214 Fabricius
215 Janssen
216 Metius
217 Brenner
218 Rheita
219 Neander
220 Piccolomini
221 Fracastorius
222 Beaumont
223 Catharina
224 Cyrillus
225 Theophilus
226 Mädler
227 Isidorus
228 Capella
229 Torricelli
230 Hypatia
231 Alfraganus
232 Delambre
233 Furnerius
234 Stevinus
235 Snellius
236 Reichenbach
237 W. Humboldt
238 Petavius
239 Santbech
240 Colombo
241 Goclenius
242 Gutenberg
243 Messier & Messier A
244 Vendelinus
245 Langrenus
246 Ansgarius
247 La Pérouse
248 Kästner

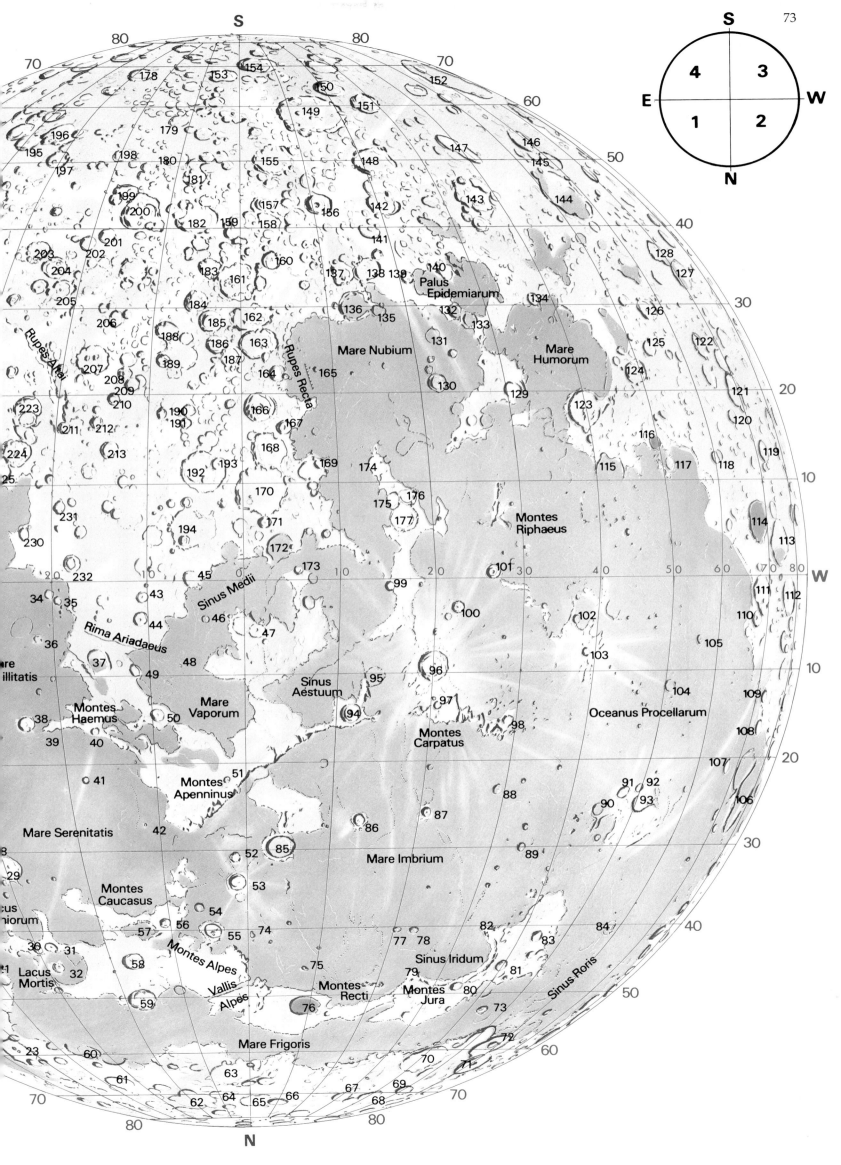

S

80   80

70   70

178   153   154   152

150

149   151   60

179

196   147   146

195   198   180   148   145   50

197   155   142   144

199   143

200   157   156

182   159   158   141   40

201   183   128

203   202   160   137   138   139   140   127

204   161   Palus

205   Epidemiarum   134   30

184   136   132   126

206   185   135   133   Mare   125

Rupes Altai   188   162   Mare Nubium   131   Humorum   122

186   163   124

207   189   187   164   165   130   129   123   121   20

208   Rupes Recta   120

209   166

223   210   190   167   116   119

211   212   191   115   117   118   10

224   213   168   169   174   Montes   114

25   192   193   Riphaeus   113

231   170   175   176   W

230   194   171   177   101   111   112

172   99   110

232   45   173   10   20   30   40   50   60   70   80

34   35   43   Sinus Medii   100   102   105   110

Rima Ariadaeus   44   46   103   109

36   48   47   96   104   10

37   49   95   Oceanus Procellarum   108

Mare   Sinus   97

illitatis   Montes   Mare   Aestuum   94   98

38   Haemus   50   Vaporum   Montes

39   40   Carpatus   20

51   91   92

41   Montes   88   90   93   107

Apenninus   87   106

42   86

Mare Serenitatis   52   85   Mare Imbrium   89   30

29   53

Montes   54

Caucasus   56   55   74   82   84   40

57   77   78   83

30   31   Montes Alpes   75   Sinus Iridum   81

58   79   Sinus Roris

Lacus   32   Montes   80

Mortis   Vallis   Recti   Montes   73   50

59   Alpes   76   Jura   72

Mare Frigoris   70

23   60   71   60

61   63   70

62   64   65   66   67   69   68   70

80   80

N

Compass rose: S (top), W (right), N (bottom), E (left); quadrants 4, 3 (top), 1, 2 (bottom)

Planetary orbits

The Earth has direct rotation – anticlockwise looking down on the North Pole – and revolves around the Sun in a similar direction, as do the other planets. Normally a planet moves slowly eastwards against the stars, like the Sun and Moon. However, the orbital period (or 'year') increases with a planet's distance from the Sun in accordance with Kepler's third law of planetary motion. (The square of the periods is proportional to the cube of the distances.) The Earth is therefore continuously overtaking the superior planets (those outside the Earth), and being overtaken by the inferior ones, Mercury and Venus. As a result, all the planets periodically appear to reverse their motions (or retrograde), moving from east to west for a while. The positions where the reversals occur are known as stationary points. With the inner planets these are also the positions of greatest elongation from the Sun, when they are most easily visible in the evening or morning sky.

The best time for observing outer planets is when they are at opposition, crossing the meridian at midnight. However, all the planetary orbits are ellipses, so the changing distances from the Earth mean that the planetary disks alter in size from one opposition to another. The best conditions occur

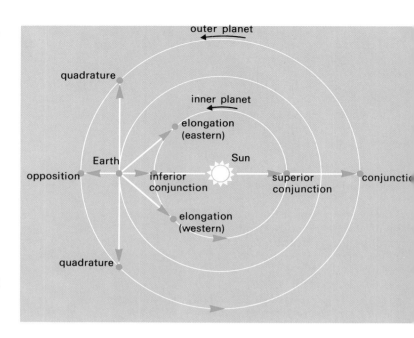

The various terms that are used to describe the positions of planets relative to the Earth and the Sun.

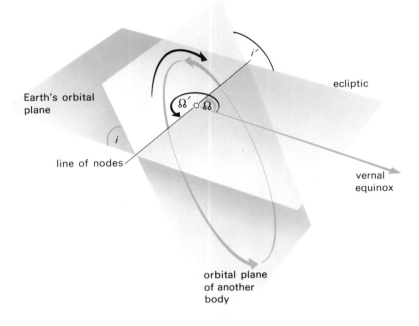

The position of an orbit in space is defined with reference to the ecliptic and to the line where the planes intersect.

All orbits in the Solar System have the Sun at one focus of the ellipse.
Below *The line joining the Sun and planet sweeps out equal areas in equal times, so the planet moves more rapidly when close to the Sun.*

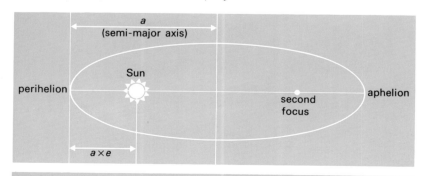

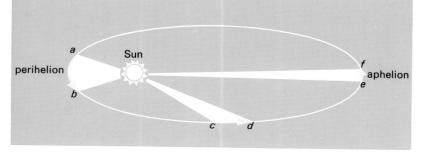

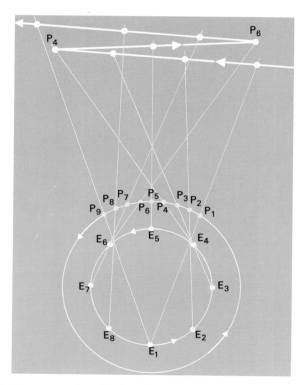

As the Earth moves in its orbit from E_1 to E_8 an outer planet appears to retrograde from P_4 to P_6. The path may frequently form a loop.

when the Earth is at aphelion (farthest from the Sun) and the outer planet is at perihelion (closest to the Sun). This is particularly important in the case of Mars, but less so with Jupiter and Saturn, where the percentage change is very much less. Similar considerations apply to the minor planets, most of which have orbits that lie between those of Mars and Jupiter. They are generally fairly faint and only readily visible around opposition. The paths of some minor planets may cross the orbit of the Earth. As they are then generally close to perihelion, their velocities are high and they may race past, rapidly changing their position in the sky from night to night.

Comets may approach the Sun from any direction, their orbits being randomly distributed, so that many have retrograde motions, unlike the planets. The orbits are also highly elongated, some so greatly that the periods can only be estimated as thousands of years. Their perihelion distances also vary greatly, some having been known to collide with the Sun, while others approach no closer than 6 or 7 astronomical units.

Planetary positions

The diagram given on this and the following page may be used to gain approximate information about the positions of the five major planets in the sky until the year 2000. The diagonal bands show the constellations that occur along the ecliptic and are marked with the standard abbreviations (page 67). Scorpius and Ophiuchus are treated together, but otherwise the width of the bands represents the length of the ecliptic within each individual constellation.

The position of the Sun is shown by the vertical line running down the centre of the diagram. Planetary elongations east or west of the Sun, measured in degrees along the ecliptic, are shwon by the graduations at the top. The order in which the planets rise may be found for any given date by reading from right to left. Planets are in conjunction with the Sun (and thus invisible) when their paths cross the central line. They remain invisible until they pass outside the zone marked by lines 10° on either side of the Sun's position. Objects with western elongations are morning objects, rising before the Sun, and those with eastern elongations are visible after sunet. For Mercury or Venus the planet is between the Earth and the Sun (at inferior conjunction) when the planet is moving westwards in the sky (from left to right). Superior conjunction is indicated by movement in the opposite direction.

An outer planet, Mars, Jupiter or Saturn, is at opposition when its path reaches 180° west of the Sun, at the right-hand edge of the diagram. It then moves into the evening sky (elongations east of the Sun) until conjunction occurs several months later.

The inferior planets show phases similar to those of the Moon, being 'full' at superior conjunction when their angular size is least. As the distance between the Earth and the planet grows smaller (towards inferior conjunction) the planet 'wanes', finally becoming invisible as a much larger, but thin, crescent. The outer planets, on the other hand, show little change in phase from 'full', except for Mars, which is close enough for the unilluminated portion to become noticeable at times.

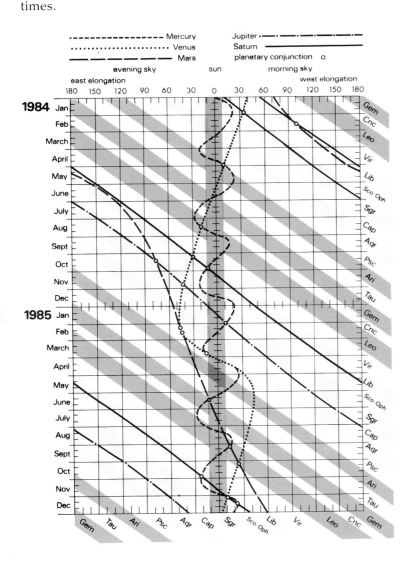

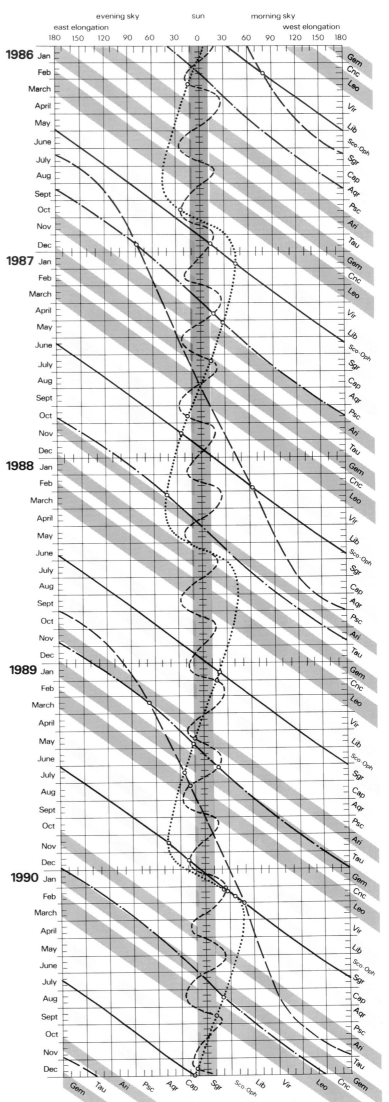

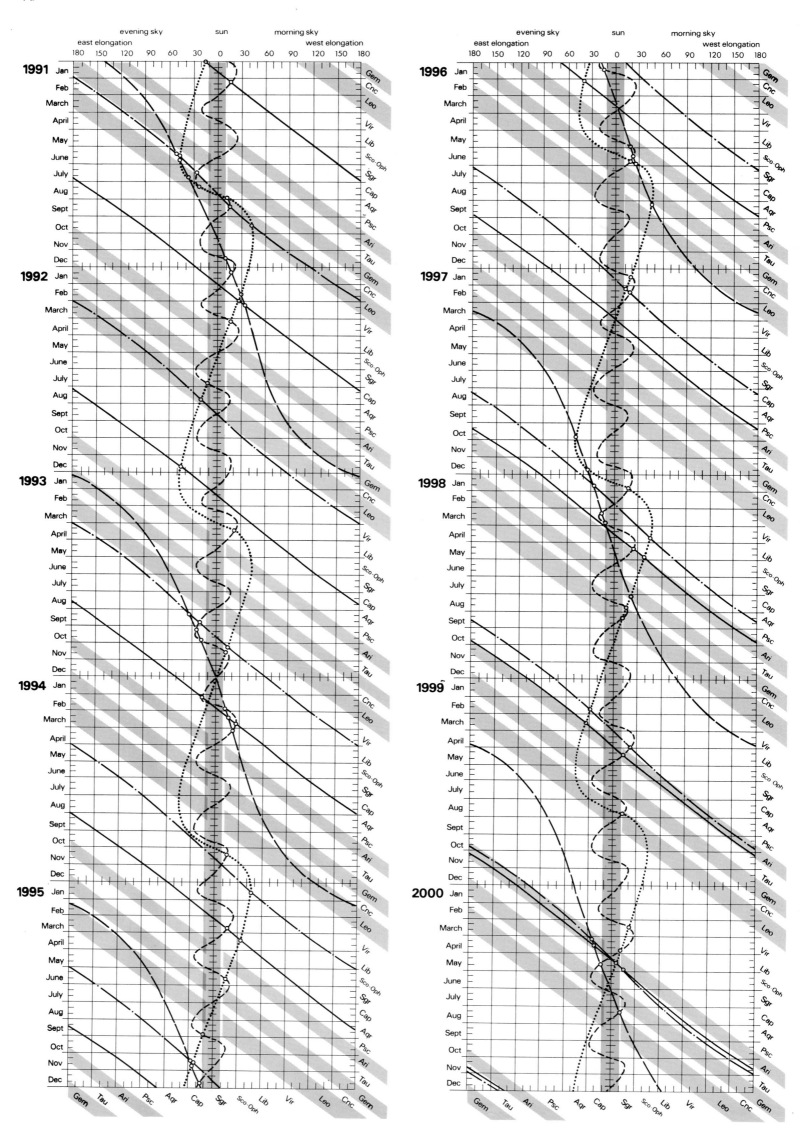

Mars

Mars is an interesting object to observe. Its rotational period is similar to the Earth's (24·6 hours), and new regions come into view during a fairly short observing session, and from night to night. The disk has an overall reddish/orange tint, but darker features are normally visible. The most prominent persist from year to year, but smaller details may change as surface material is moved from one area to another by the winds. Sometimes wide-spread dust storms may arise, covering a large area with a yellowish veil. On occasions, indeed, these storms may develop into planet-wide disturbances, hiding the whole surface beneath featureless clouds of dust.

The polar ice caps are the brightest areas, but only one is seen at a time owing to the tilt of the rotational axis of Mars. They slowly change in size with the progress of the martian seasons. Their decay in spring and summer may often be observed, but details of their spread are frequently hidden by a 'polar hood' of cloud that develops in the martian autumn. Other clouds may sometimes be seen elsewhere on the surface, most especially on the morning terminator, where they persist until dispersed by the warmth of the Sun.

Drawings showing the shrinking of the south polar cap of Mars.

The oppositions of Mars in 1986 and 1988 are equally favourable. That in 1980 was the worst that can occur.

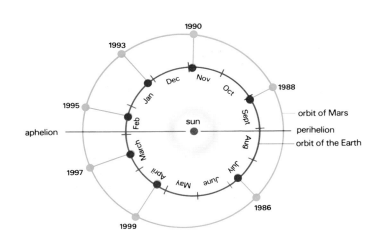

Jupiter

The most noticeable markings on the cloud-covered surface of Jupiter are the dark belts and polar regions, and the intervening bright zones. These all have a wealth of finer detail in the form of innumerable streaks and spots, which are continually changing in shape and intensity. The most famous feature, the Great Red Spot, has been visible for at least 300 years but has altered very considerably during that time, and appears to be slowly decaying. The planet's fast rotation (9ʰ 50ᵐ approximately, for the equatorial regions) causes a distinct change to become apparent in a very short time, so drawings must be made quickly if they are to be accurate.

Almost as fascinating at the planet itself are the four main satellites, Io, Europa, Ganymede and Callisto. They are visible in even the smallest pair of binoculars. With somewhat larger instruments they may be observed crossing the planet's disk (transits), or their shadows may be seen to do the same (shadow transits). They may be hidden by Jupiter itself (occultations) or else disappear into its shadow (eclipses).

An amateur drawing of Jupiter showing complex details on the disk and a shadow transit.

Jupiter's belts (B), polar regions (PR) and zones (Z):

E = Equatorial;

N = North;

S = South;

T = Temperate;

Tr = Tropical.

GRS = Great Red Spot.

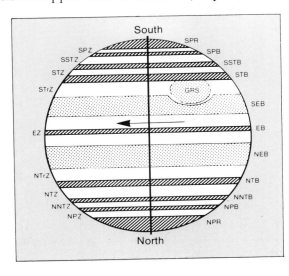

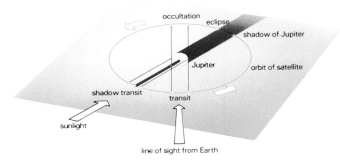

An idealized situation illustrating the occurrence of Jupiter's satellite phenomena.

Saturn

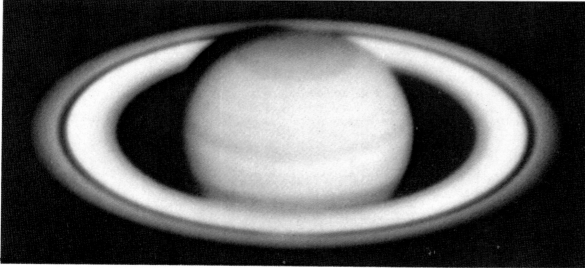

This composite photograph from Earth shows about the same amount of detail as can normally be seen with small telescopes.

26.4°

ecliptic

Saturn has a banded appearance similar to that of Jupiter, with bright zones and dark belts. Other features are rare – they are hidden by an overlying haze – but observations become all the more important when they are visible. The planet compensates for this lack of detail with its magnificent rings. Two of these, the A (outer) and B Rings are easily visible, separated by the Cassini Division. Another ring, the C (or Crêpe) Ring inside the B Ring, is more difficult to see. Although the rings are very thin (hundreds of metres at the most), the shadow that they cast onto the planet is frequently visible. (The shadow of the planet on the rings is usually present, although difficult to see when the Earth is close to the plane of the rings.)

Like Jupiter, Saturn has several satellites that are visible in small telescopes. Titan, the largest satellite in the Solar System (both it and Jupiter's Ganymede exceed the size of Mercury), is usually a little below magnitude 8.

Saturn has a high inclination to the ecliptic but twice in the Saturnian 'year' the ring is seen edge-on from Earth, when it disappears.

Other planets

Venus is the most interesting of the remaining planets. It shows great changes in size and appearance as it orbits the Sun, and the crescent phase may be seen with a good pair of binoculars. It may become very brilliant (about magnitude -4), and is sometimes observed in daylight to lessen the effects of glare. Unfortunately its surface is permanently shrouded in dense clouds and the tops of these show very few features. Brighter 'cusp caps' and various darker shadings are sometimes visible.

Mercury is not easy to see as it is always so close to the Sun. It is best to search for it when it is at elongation or when close to another planet in the sky. (When the two planets' paths cross on the diagram on pp. 75–6). It does shows changes of phase, like Venus, but its disk is too small for any distinct features to be visible.

Uranus, the planet beyond Saturn, is just at the limit of naked-eye visibility, but can easily be seen in binoculars. It shows a pale blue/green disk, but only the largest telescopes and the keenest eyesight can make out faint belts. It is unique among the planets in that its rotational axis lies nearly in the orbital plane – it is actually tipped over by 98°. At times the poles may therefore point almost directly towards the Sun.

Even farther out than Uranus, Neptune (the last of the four 'gas giants') comes to about magnitude 8 at opposition, so is just visible in moderate binoculars, if one knows where to look. No details are visible on the tiny disk.

Pluto is normally the outermost planet, but at present is closer to the Sun than Neptune, owing to its very eccentric orbit. It is very small and very faint (about magnitude 15 at opposition) so it needs a large telescope and detailed charts for it to be even located. None of the satellites of the outer planets Uranus (5), Neptune (2) or Pluto (1) are detectable with small telescopes.

Between the orbits of Mars and Jupiter lie those of the minor planets (sometimes known as asteroids from their likeness to tiny stars). Several thousand are known and this is doubtless only a small part of the whole population. All are small; the largest, Ceres, only having a diameter of about 1000 km. Most are very faint, but approximately twenty may exceed magnitude 10 at opposition.

The paths of Uranus (below) and Neptune (above).

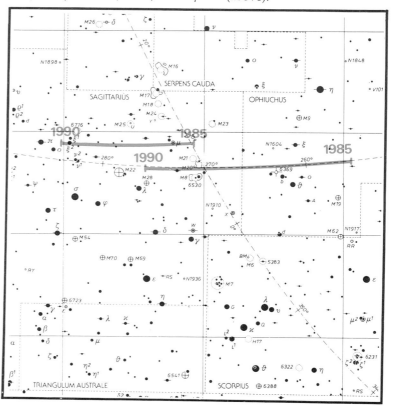

Comets and Meteors

Comets pose many problems for astronomers, not least because most are quite unpredictable, and may appear in any part of the sky. Some remain close to the Sun and are difficult to study in any detail. A few may become very prominent and bright as they round the Sun, before dwindling again into obscurity as they recede into the outer Solar System. Rarely, they may be so bright that they are visible in daylight. Those comets with known paths are generally much fainter and less spectacular, which is why Comet Halley excites such interest: it is fairly bright and quite predictable.

A comet's actual appearance is never certain. All comets have a head, the coma, formed from material given off by cometary body, which consists of frozen gases and dust particles. Some objects may show no more than this, remaining just a faint fuzzy patch. Others grow tails, some mere wisps of gas, and others highly spectacular trails of gas and dust. The coma sometimes shows a brilliant point of light, the nucleus, at its centre.

Comets waste away at each return, but the dust particles remain in orbit and gradually become dispersed with time. When these particles encounter the Earth's atmosphere, they burn up in a brief flash as meteors. Most occur randomly (sporadics), but several times a year the Earth passes through denser streams which give rise to meteor showers. Some of these are definitely linked with known comets – the Orionids with Halley's Comet, for example. In other cases the parent comet has never been recorded. The numbers of meteors during showers may vary greatly, although a few showers such as the Perseids are reasonably consistent and show moderately high rates. The Leonids are a spectacular exception. Normally very weak, approximately every 33 years (the orbital period of the original parent body) they may produce phenomenal displays. In 1966 the (hourly) rate rose to about 150 000 and persisted at that level for about 20 minutes. Very bright meteors (>mag.-5) are known as fireballs.

Comet West shows two tails in this photograph: the narrow gas tail, pointing directly away from the Sun, and the broad tail of dust spread along the comet's orbit.

Principal meteor showers*

shower	date of maximum	normal limits	ZHR† at max	position of radiant			remarks
				right ascension h m		declination °	
Quadrantids	Jan. 4	Jan. 1–6	80	15	30	+50	Blue meteors with fine trains – many faint shower members.
η-Aquarids	May 5	May 1–8	40	22	27	00	Meteors with persistent trains.
δ-Aquarids	July 28	July 15–Aug. 15	35	22	39	00	Double radiant. Meteors with long paths.
				22	36	−17	
Perseids	Aug. 12	July 25–Aug. 18	100	03	08	+58	Fine shower, rich in bright meteors with persistent trains.
Orionids	Oct. 21	Oct. 16–26	20	06	27	+15	Meteors with persistent trains.
Taurids	Nov. 8	Oct 20–Nov. 30	12	03	47	+14	Double radiant. Brilliant meteors.
				03	47	+22	
Leonids	Nov. 17	Nov. 15–19	10	10	11	+22	Unpredictable shower. A ZHR of about 10 is normal but every 33.33 years there is a chance of much higher activity. Spectacular displays occurred in 1799, 1833, 1866, and 1966 – when a ZHR of around 150 000 was maintained for about 20 minutes!
Geminids	Dec. 14	Dec. 7–15	60	07	31	+32	

* For a more comprehensive list (including many minor showers) see the annual *Handbook of the British Astronomical Association*.

† The ZHR or Zenithal Hourly Rate is the computed hourly rate for an observer for whom the radiant is on the zenith. (The actual rates may vary considerably from year to year and the values shown are only in indication of the general level of activity.)

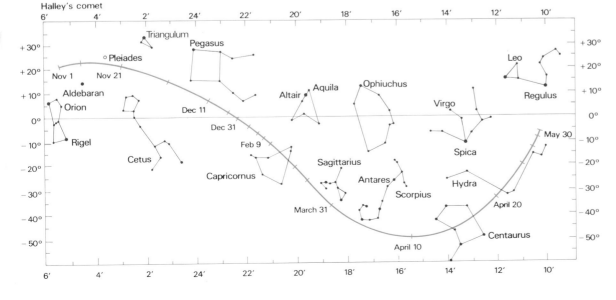

The orbits of comets may be retrograde for a long period and take them well away from the ecliptic, as in the case of Halley's Comet in 1985–6.

Journals and Magazines

Astronomy, AstroMedia Corp., PO Box 92788, Milwaukee, Wisconsin (monthly)

Journal, British Astronomical Association, Burlington House, Piccadilly, London W1V 0NL (bimonthly)

New Scientist, London (frequent astronomical articles, weekly)

Popular Astronomy, Junior Astronomical Society, 58 Vaughan Gardens, Ilford, Essex 1G1 3PD (quarterly)

Quarterly Journal, Royal Astronomical Society, Burlington House, Piccadilly, London W1V 0NL (quarterly)

Sky & Telescope, Sky Publishing, 49 Bay State Road, Cambridge, Mass 02138 (monthly)

Scientific American, New York (frequent astronomical articles, monthly)

The Astronomer, 1 Manor Park, Wellingborough, Northants NN8 3QQ (amateur observations, monthly)

Bibliography
General Books

Allen, R. H., *Star Names, Their Lore and Meaning*, Dover, New York, 1963.

Beatty, J. K., O'Leary, B. and Chaikin, A., *The New Solar System*, 2nd edn, Cambridge University Press, 1983.

Bok, B. J. & Bok, P., *The Milky Way*, 5th edn, Harvard University Press, Cambridge, Mass. 1981.

Davies, P. C. W., *Space and Time in the Modern Universe*, Cambridge University Press, Cambridge, 1977.

Ferris, T., *The Red Limit*, Corgi Books, London, 1979.

Harrison, E. R., *Cosmology: The Science of the Universe*, Cambridge University Press, 1981.

Hey, J. S., *The Radio Universe*, 2nd edn, Pergamon, Oxford, 1975.

Illingworth, V., ed., *The Macmillan Dictionary of Astronomy*, Macmillan, London, 1979.

Kaufmann, W.J., *The Cosmic Frontiers of General Relativity*, Penguin, London, 1979.

Learner, R., *Astronomy through the Telescope*, Evans, London, 1981.

Ley, M., *Watchers of the Skies*, Viking Press, New York, 1963.

Mitton, S., *Daytime Star*, Faber, London, 1981.

—, *Exploring the Galaxies*, Faber, London, 1976.

Morrison, D., *Voyages to Saturn*, NASA, Washington, 1982.

—, & Samz, J., *Voyage to Jupiter*, NASA, Washington, 1980.

Nicolson, I., *Astronomy, a Dictionary of Space and the Universe*, Arrow Books, London, 1977.

—, *The Sun*, Mitchell Beazley, London, 1982.

Shipman, H. L., *Black Holes, Quasars, and the Universe*, 2nd ed., Houghton Mifflin, Boston, Mass., 1980.

Silk, J., *The Big Bang*, Freeman, San Francisco, 1980.

Smith, F. G., *Radio Astronomy*, 4th edn, Penguin, London, 1974.

Waugh, A. E., *Sundials*, Dover, New York, 1973.

Whitney, C. A., *The Discovery of Our Galaxy*, Alfred A. Knopf., New York, 1971.

Practical Books and Publications

American Association of Variable Star Observers, *AAVSO Variable Star Atlas*, Sky Publishing, Cambridge, Mass., 1980.

Baxter, W. M., *The Sun and the Amateur Astronomer*, David & Charles, Newton Abbot, 1972.

British Astronomical Association, *Guide for Observers of the Moon*, London, 1974.

—, *Handbook.*, London, annually

—, *Satellite Observers' Manual*, London, 1974.

—, *Star Charts*, London, 1981.

Burnham, R., *Burnham's Celestial Handbook*, (3 vols), Dover, New York, 1978.

Chartrand, Mark, R., *Amateur Astronomy Pocket Skyguide*, Newnes Books, London (Golden Press, New York), 1984.

Couteau, P., *Observing Visual Double Stars*, MIT Press, London, 1981.

Duffett-Smith, *Practical Astronomy with your Calculator*, 2nd edn, Cambridge University Press, 1981.

Eastman Kodak, Co., *Astrophotography Basics*, Publication AC–48, Rochester, NY, 1980.

Jones, A., *Mathematical Astronomy with a Pocket Calculator*, David & Charles, Newton Abbott, 1978.

Jones, K. G., Messier's *Nebulae and Star Clusters*, Faber, London, 1968.

King-Hele, D., *Observing Earth Satellites*, Macmillan, London, 1983.

Klepesta, J. and Rukl. A., *Constellations*, Hamlyn, London, 1969.

Mallas, J. H. & Kreimer, E., *The Messier Album*, Cambridge U. P., Cambridge, 1978.

Mayall, N. & Mayall, M., *Skyshooting – Photography for Amateur Astronomers*, Dover, New York, 1968.

Moore, P., ed., *Practical Amateur Astronomy*, 4th edn, Lutterworth Press, Guildford, 1975.

Norton, A. P., *Norton's Star Atlas*, 17th edn, ed. Satterthwaite, G. S., Gall & Inglis, Edinburgh, 1978.

Ronan, C. A., ed., *Amateur Astronomy*, Newnes Books, London, 1984.

Roth, G. D., *Handbook for Planet Observers*, Faber and Faber, London.

Royal Astronomical Society of Canada, *Observer's Handbook*, Toronto, Ontario (annually).

Rukl, A., *Moon, Mars and Venus*, Hamlyn, London, 1976.

Sidgwick, J. B., *Amateur Astronomer's Handbook*, (4th edn, ed. Muirden, J.), Pelham, London, 1979.

Sidgwick, J. B., *Observational Astronomy for Amateurs*, (4th edn, ed. Muirden, J.), Pelham, London 1982.

Texereau, J., *How to Make a Telescope*, Doubleday, New York, 1963.

Tirion, W., *Sky Atlas 2000.0*, Sky Publishing, Cambridge, Mass., 1981.

Societies
British Organisations

British Astronomical Association, Burlington House, Piccadilly, London W1V 0NL

British Interplanetary Society, 27–29 South Lambeth Road, London SW8 1SZ

Junior Astronomical Society, 58 Vaughan Gardens, Ilford, Essex 1G1 3PD

Royal Astronomical Society, Burlington House, Piccadilly, London W1V 0NL

North American organisations

American Association of Variable Star Observers (AAVSO) – 187 Concord Avenue, Cambridge, Massachusetts 02138

American Meteor Society – Dept of Physics and Astronomy, SUNY, Genesco, NY, 14454

Association of Lunar and Planetary Observers (ALPO) – Box 3AZ, University Park, New Mexico 88003

Astronomical League – P.O. Box 12821, Tucson, Arizona 85732 (for addresses of local societies)

Astronomical Society of the Pacific – 1290 24th Ave., San Francisco, California 94122

Royal Astronomical Society of Canada – 136 Dupont Street, Toronto, Ontario M5R 1Vs (20 Centres throughout Canada)

Western Amateur Astronomers – A. McDermott (Secretary), P.O. Box 2316, Palm Desert, California 92261 (for addresses of local societies)

Other organisations

Astronomical Society of New South Wales – P.O. Box 208, Eastwood, New South Wales 2122, Australia

Astronomical Society of South Australia – P.O. Box 199, Adelaide, South Australia 501, Australia

Astronomical Society of Southern Africa – c/o South African Astronomical Observatory, P.O. Box 9, Observatory, 7935, Cape, Republic of South Africa

Astronomical Society of Victoria – P.O. Box 1059J, Melbourne, Victoria 3001, Australia

British Astronomical Association (New South Wales Branch) – Sydney Observatory, Sydney, New South Wales, 2001, Australia

Royal Astronomical Society of New Zealand – P.O. Box 3181, Wellington C1, New Zealand.